MAKING IT

by
Jo Ann Mills

QUALITY PUBLICATIONS
P.O. BOX 1060
ABILENE, TEXAS 79604
(915) 677-6262

Copyright © Jo Ann Mills 1986

ISBN: 089137-439-6

DEDICATION

This book is dedicated to Bob, my husband and best friend, to Robby and Mitch, my sons, without whom I could not have *Made It.*

Agape love is "never haughty or selfish or rude. Love does not demand its own way. It is not irritable or touchy. It does not hold grudges and *(love) will hardly even notice when others do it wrong"* (*The Living Bible,* 1 Corinthians 13:5) TBL.

PERMISSIONS

"Calm Repose" by Robert Browning, used by permission from Random House, Inc. Alfred A. Knoff, Inc.

Lauer, Robert H. Editorial section from *Modern Secretary* by Dr.Lauer, United States International University, San Diego, CA, used by permission from Dr. Lauer.

Choate, Betty B. "Growing Old in Love," *Love Poems;* Used by permission of author Betty Choate.

Rice, Helen Steiner, "The Meaning of True Love," *The Greatest of These is Love*, is used by permission of Dr. Kauffman, The Foundation for Christian Living.

Verses marked TBL are taken from *The Living Bible*, copyright, 1971, by Tyndale House Publishers, Wheaton, IL.

Guenther, Louis H. "Life's Seasons." Permission granted to use father's poem by son, Stephen C. Guenther.

TABLE OF CONTENTS

Page

Introduction 1
    Life Seasons 5

Chapter I
    Great Expectations and Wild Dreams 7
    The Meaning of True Love 14
    Study Questions 15

Chapter II
    In Staying in Love With Mate 17
    Study Questions 21

Chapter III
    In Doing and Not Worrying 23
    Study Questions 26

Chapter IV
    In Matters of Raising Children 27
    "If" by Rudyard Kipling 29
    Study Questions 34

Chapter V
    Making It In Financial Matters 37
    Study Questions 44

Chapter VI
    In Playing The Proper Role As a Wife
        in Sexual Matters 47
    Growing Old In Love 53
    Study Questions 55

Chapter VII

    In Playing the Proper Role as a Wife

        in Headship-Submission 57

    Study Questions 62

Chapter VIII

    In Developing the "C" Characteristics of Marriage 63

        The Communicators 63

        The Committed 64

        The Considerate 65

        The Collaborators 65

        The Courageous 66

        The Christians 67

    Study Questions 68

Chapter IX

    In Saving the Marriage That is Failing 69

    Study Questions 75

Chapter X

    In Time When Children Leave Home 77

    An Old Can Full of Coins 78

    Study Questions 83

Chapter XI

    In Time When Illness Strikes a Love One 85

    Study Questions 88

    Calm Repose or Grow Old With Me 88

Chapter XII

    In Hurting Less and Loving More 91

    Study Questions 102

Chapter XIII

Conclusion 103
Study Questions 107

Bibliography 108

INTRODUCTION

No single factor does more to give a marriage joy or keep it both a venture and an adventure, in mutual fulfillment, than shared commitment in finding out how to serve God. Church related activities bring marriage partners closer. To be asked to spend one's life together with another person is one of the greatest honors in life. We must understand love to make marriage work, and only those who seek God's will can learn true agape love — a love which is unselfish and serving. Model the role you want followed. If you desire to have an unselfish and serving love, you must be unselfish and serving. "One flesh" is ultimate achievement for marital partners. However, it must be remembered that the "one flesh" relationship is more comprehensive than a sexual relationship, although sex is a part of that "one flesh" relationship.

The greatest compliment a wife can give to her husband is found in her pledge "to love him till death do us part," because with this pledge she indicates that she will also "love God until death takes her away from that mate."

The request every good wife should make of her husband is "don't try to understand me — just love me!" To "love me" would imply that there should be shared confidences, mutual trust and faith, and shared safe and secure environment. If the mates grant each other these things, then the relationship will mature as the couples go from the *spring* to the *winter* and then those dear friends, those partners in life, can reach the end of their lives stating to themselves and to others, "We have made it!"

This work is intended to encourage young women to follow the teachings of Titus 2:4-5: "That they be in behavior as becometh holiness . . ."; Titus 3:2 "be gentle, shewing all meekness unto all men."

The purpose of the writer was to begin, in a note-taking process, a work which was patterned after 30 years of married life, to take the reader through the seasons of the adulthood of life from the marriage altar to the eventual separation by death. In doing so, the writer realized that development of a good marriage relationship continued along with all the opportunities of life. Awareness made the journey through those seasons of adulthood easier.

With this in mind, I began praying that God would direct my thoughts and studies and my talents and use them in the way He would have them used. After several weeks, thoughts began

1

to form in my mind and I was urged to write them down lest I forget. So, I began a system of intensive entries in both my diary and journal. Still, I feel there have been many thoughts that have come and then slipped away, which should have been recorded; however, those thoughts are now lost to me. Maybe they will return and fall into the proper place at the proper time, acquiring the space that would be deserved.

The outline for the topics to be covered serving as divisions are:

I. Great Expectations and Wild Dreams

II. In Staying in Love With Mate

III. In Doing and Not Worrying

IV. In Matters of Raising Children

V. In Financial Matters

VI. In Playing the Proper Role As Wife In Sexual Matters

VII. In Playing Proper Role As Wife in Headship-Submission

VIII. In Developing the "C" Characteristics of Marriage

IX. In Saving the Marriage That is Failing

X. In Time When Children Leave Home

XI. In Time When Illness Strikes a Love One

XII. In Hurting Less and Loving More

XIII. Conclusion

Just as the stages of life are referred to as seasons, so are the stages of a marriage when everything is new and much adjustment takes priority; summertime is the season of raising our children and watching them grow as we ourselves grow and adjust further; autumn is the time when everything seems to be at its fullest radiance — the children are grown, the relationship merges back so that two people can find more time for themselves and explore the new brilliance of a personality made wiser by years of experiences and discipline and growth; and then the winter time is the time when life nears its last stages and we begin to understand and blend and the soul comes into harmony with the situations.

In this work I will include instances outside my family upon which I will have to rely to bring more truth to light as examples of how others have *made it* through perilous times because there are instances that should be covered in *making it* which have not been a part of my own experiences. All people's lives are different, even though most idealistic Christian families generally try to conform to an overall pattern which is nearly the same. The implication is not classism, I prefer not to classify — I prefer to state that all people who marry, whether they are from the very poor or the very rich in material blessings, should have one purpose in mind when they marry, and that purpose should be that they are going to *make it* or they should not marry. Trial and error in learning lessons in life or experience at success and failure are not prerequisites for all things — especially not marriage. Dating should have provided the trial and error basis for finding someone with whom one can build a lasting relationship — not marriage and re-marriage. Marriage should be a bond, a blending together of two people into one. Perhaps several good definitions of marriage and scriptures should be referred to at this time.

"Wherefore they are no more twain, but one flesh. What therefore God hath joined together, let not man put asunder" (Matthew 19:6). Jesus taught that marriage was a relationship that mankind should leave alone — a relationship that should be nourished and left to grow. Becoming one flesh is not just a state of marriage, it is a bonding together of two people, male and female, husband and wife. Many couples go through a ceremony, but sometime, somewhere along the way, they have quit being married in their minds and hearts. They may never go for a divorce, continue to live in the same house, but will never live up to God' description of what marriage is to be.

Marriage is a lifetime contract according to Romans 7:1-4; marriage is an idealistic state of being into which men and women are drawn, not because it's expected of them, or the thing to do, but because there is a need in man to reach this state. Life is not easy; it is very difficult to travel through the stages of our lives alone. But it must be remembered that marriage is not a state in which two persons find each other and live happily ever after as we read about in the fairy-tale romance stories. Crisis will occur, but if good and godly husbands and wives pattern themselves after the marriage design mentioned in Genesis 2 whereby the participant's attitudes made the marriage become a beautiful spiritual relationship, then a truly lasting marriage will evolve.

Marriage is a helping, serving, edifying, building, and encouraging enterprise in which one engages. Galatians 5:13 is a statement calling for us to serve one another as free people (. . . "ye have been called unto liberty; only use not liberty for an occasion to the flesh, but by love serve one another"). Also, in Paul's writings he taught that we should be kind to one another, forgiving, even as God has forgiven us. This teaches living in love by being kind, tenderhearted and forgiving. This is exactly what one is called upon to do on a continual basis in marriage. When one enters into a business for himself and operates that business within the law of the land, then that one is operating a free enterprise. When one enters into a marriage and operates within that marriage within the laws set up by God, then that one is operating a selfless enterprise. This selfless enterprise has to come from the partners involved in that enterprise.

A married couple's development grows and continues to grow along with the opportunities shared as the couple proceed through the seasons of married life. A keen awareness of a marital partner's needs makes the journey through the seasons easier.

One scripture that forever comes to my mind when I relate how I made it through all the seasons of married life thus far is from Philippians 2:14 — "Do all things without murmurings or disputing."

LIFE'S SEASONS

Life is like the seasons
    Each one its changes bring
A fertile seed takes root and grows
    Thus youth is like the Spring
Maturity comes in Summer
    As we work and play and sing,
In the Fall we gather harvest
    from the deeds we sowed, and then
All too soon it's Winter
    And our eyes hve grown quite dim,
Have faith no need to worry
    'Tis not the end of everything
For our souls will be returned again
    To Heaven, where God is king.

Louis H. Guenther

Chapter I

GREAT EXPECTATIONS
AND WILD DREAMS

The first years of marriage are probably the most difficult years with problems as: being realistic and not inclined to fantasy or romantic inclinations of what marriage is all about; money management; sex; interest; and, decisions on whether there should be any children.

The *20th Century Christian* magazine submitted a plan for strength which the writer felt very appropriate for entry into this work. In order for the couple to meet the challenges during the first three years of married life, the couple should:[1]

1. Spend time together and become truly acquainted.

2. Recognize the marriage as being their marriage.

3. Face problems as money management, sexual problems, whether to have children as directly and optimistically as possible.

I don't ever remember my marriage as being blissful, or a storybook, fanciful thing as portrayed in the movies I had seen or books I had read. I do remember many good things as well as recall many bad things which occurred during the course of our marriage. But I can say this, that from the beginning, our marriage never faced unfaithfulness by either party and I think I know the reason. We were committed to one another and almost from the point of time when our friends' marriages started to get a little shaky and uncertain, we

7

entered into another commitment — one which included God and His will. I remember this well because this was when I became a Christian. Our children were ages 7 and 4. Without this commitment, we would have not made it. Our associations became different, our lifestyle changed, and our purposes and goals became more unified.

I suppose the first thing it takes to make sure that you get on the right foot to making things work would be to get the right mate in the beginning. God planned that a God-fearing mother raise a very special person just for me and I believe this with all my heart and I thank Him daily that He directed the lives which moved me closer to the plan that He had in mind just for me! The boyfriend I had as a young teenager, whom I dated off and on throughout my high school and part of my college years, and whom my family and everyone else thought I would eventually marry, would have been a disastrous choice and would have eventually resulted in a crushing impact upon my life, and God knew that! I remember this fellow of mine as a superstar college athlete and I thought he was great, but my feelings of his greatness began to wane when I learned he had been stealing exams from a college reproduction room and selling them. He and my husband used to have sitting contests to see which one of them would outlast the other when both happened to come calling at my home. There could have been a toss up as to whom I might decide to let monopolize my time. Thank God I chose rightly. Here it is, 30 years after the fact and I am comfortable in my life, never taking happiness for granted, but knowing that I am assured that I will never have more than I can bear as a burden, and that I don't have to worry as I share excitement in life, even as my mate and I pass from the Fall season of life. Choices are very important, young women, because you will have to live with the choices you make — good or bad. Be sure that you put God in your life so that you will make the right ones. The way to do this is by prayer and supplication to God's will. (Philippians 4:6 "Be careful for nothing; but in everything by prayer and supplication with thanksgiving let your requests be made known unto God.")

Just the other day, I said to my husband, "If I just knew 20 years ago what I know today, my life would have been a lot easier," and the topic of our discussion was annuities and insurance against social security and retirement funds.

My husband and I began our marriage with $50 in cash, a guaranteed G.I. education bill payment of approximately $135 monthly, and $20 monthly in laundry money, which was part of his athletic scholarship. We were both in college at the time, with Him lacking three full years for completion of his studies. However, we both came from humble surroundings, did not expect much and so we knew not felt, we could make it because we had love. Funny how you never second-guess or look back and put things on a scale, weigh them out on what will balance with what, when you are young and making decisions — you just make the decision and learn to live with it. So, on a brisk cold December day, we pledged our vows to one another in my parents' home. We had a small wedding party with only about 20 guests in attendance on that Sunday afternoon. We decided right away that our $50 would not take us as far as San Antonio, so we traveled only a short distance to spend our wedding night. I even had my first experience at being a good wife when we discovered that in his excitement, my new husband had brought only one pair of undershorts with him, which I had to wash out to be worn the next day. Having never been with a man on this basis before, it is needless to say that I was very uncomfortable at first. Gentleness and patience had their beginnings at this time and progressed on throughout the marriage.

Upon returning from our brief two-day honeymoon to occupy a very small two room apartment, in which we remained for 21 months, we shared some interesting, sad, and happy times learning that two different people can occasionally harmonize. Then we moved, with Bob dropping out of college and going to work full-time to support our family, as our first son arrived approximately 1 year and 10 months following our marriage, as was the custom in the good old days.

While we were in that unique, doll-scaled apartment, where one could lie on the bed and open the front door, I learned many things. Trial and error in making my first pie crust was an ordeal that Bob and I laugh at until this day. I had purchased one of those package mixes that looks like a square of margarine and proceeded to try and make a pie crust like the one which appeared on the label. Try as I did, the shape would not fit the pan. Finally, I began crying because my efforts were so frustrating and futile. Bob heard me and came to my rescue — he proceeded to take the task in hand and it appeared as if he had the determination to make it work. I stepped back and watched. The pan sat empty. In desperation and anger, Bob stepped the two steps from the cabinet to the back door, opened it, and hurled the dough into the air like a Frizbee. I watched my crust spinning through the air and finally flop disgracefully onto a pile of dead leaves on the compost pile. I went to the place where it fell, gave it a proper burial, covering it with loose leaves and brush.

Bob was always going to help me do something by showing me how — somehow those helping sessions always ended up with me in "stitches with laughter" and his being miffed by his inability to perform the task: like the time he was going to help me learn to sew.

"Oh, I've seen Mama do that a thousand times," he said, "now let's just put this right here and this right here," and away we would go. We cut one side of the material with the grain going "north" and the other side with the grain going "south." Now, anyone who knows anything about sewing knows that you just don't do that unless you like two-tone garments. Also, I've since learned you don't cut material crosswise — but we did that, too, rather cleverly, I might add. Needless to say, there was much trial and error in any project we attempted together, but even though the material was wasted, the efforts at learning to work cooperatively were not. I look back at these as growing moments and we shared many growing moments, faced many frustrations, but we matured in our relationship with one another. Our first big disagreement came with the summer when it was very hot and humid. I had my car pool chauffer let me off at the usual place, which happened to be at a busy intersection on the hot pavement. I waited and waited for what seemed like an hour and a half and Bob, who was coming from the oil fields, where he had gotten summer work, was to pick me up. Then he and his riders came breezing up, laughing and joking. I was boiling at that point and getting in the car between two dirty sweaty men who smelled of grease and stale cigarettes made me even more uncomfortable. My underclothes were sticking to my body and sweat trickled down my neck and back and my mind was clouded with my discomfort. As I look back now, I know that I was the cause of this argument, because I had lacked one of the first qualities of a true Christian — patience (Romans 12:12; Romans 2:4; 1 Corinthians 13:4; 2 Corinthians 6:6; Colossians 3:12; James 5:11). All of these scriptures now teach me that to be a Christian I must be patient or longsuffering.

I don't remember his ever having left me waiting on a corner in the heat of summer any more after this, but I do remember the argument which ensued and which caused a faction of bitterness between us. We continued to learn that small inconveniences which occur in marriage can blow up into large arguments and much fury can pass between two otherwise agreeing partners and this could be left alone to build a "wall" forcing those partners apart if allowed to continue.

Another big and lasting quarrel which was brought on by an action which was as unprovoked by me as any I could recall, but one which Bob used as his "weapon" from time to time at his convenience for about seven years of our marriage, occurred during the second year of marriage. We had been attending a large church for some time during our marriage, and this Sunday should have been no different than any other Sunday, but my boss who had resigned from a job where he had been director in charge of personnel and left to take more lucrative employment elsewhere, saw me from a distance in the lobby of the building and came heralding over with exclamation in his eyes and sound of rejoicing in his voice and planted a big kiss right on my cheek near my neck and ear. Ooh! The roof should come down so hard! Here I was, out to my toes with the extra contour caused by being seven months pregnant and another man, of all men, my ex-boss, should smack me — in front of my husband, yet! I was never the belle of the office force where I worked, nor had I ever been flirty or flippant with any personnel; I was just a young woman who smiled a lot, tried to be pleasant at all times to my co-workers, who had been married only a year and nine months, and trying to make a days' wage so my husband could stay in college and get his education so he could make the day's wage. I was as embarrassed as anyone could be over the incident as the greeting was totally surprising to me. My only explanation to Bob was (and believe me I was required to explain more than once) that he was indeed happy to see me again and apparently "believed in the greeting of one another with a holy kiss." However, I knew that my mate was jealous before I married him and this was one of those traits that most men manage to exhibit, and possibly many women, that requires much time and trust and exemplification of faithfulness to remove the trait and have other traits which upbuild character replace it. Even now, ever so slightly, my dear sweet mate enjoys ribbing me by remembering the incident, but I think he is truly trying to flatter me into thinking that after all these years, anyone's slight attention to me matters to him. However, now, using the wisdom which time has given me, I really wonder what must have gone through his mind at that particular time and wonder if he ever seriously thought that all those stories people tell about the boss chasing the secretaries around the desk was true. And in incidents like this, and perhaps others that occur, is found the foundation for growth of mutual trust. For in the mutual trust one knows that he is trustworthy and another must know that also in order to perfect that trust. Thereby, we have mutual trust which is a key element in *Making It.* In situations of learning and growth, as just mentioned, my mate and I were charter members of the 'Mills' Funny Farm.'

Perhaps one of the most important things for a couple to remember is that they must find peace with one another, which includes forgiveness, and understanding (Mark 9:50; Romans 14:19; 1 Corinthians 13:5). As hard as newly married mates work to please

11

the other mate, often it is very difficult even if the mate understands the commitment which was made to the other when they were married. We will see enough people "despitefully use" our mates in life, so we should make sure that we do not turn out to be one of these "users." After we establish the peace with one another, then we can get on with the service that we owe to one another (Galatians 5:13; Philippians 2:5-7; Hebrews 13:16). The husband should begin to understand that you mean it when you say to him, "Here I am, tell me, let me help you, or you can believe in me." When everyone else out there is criticizing and demeaning, the wife needs to be there serving and let her husband know by rendering agape service. More will be explained on this type of service later in this book. We should encourage one another daily (Hebrews 3:13, 10:24) in marriage just as we do in church.

True, we had some bad times, but we have certainly had some good times, too. As a matter of fact, sometimes we came out of sad situations laughing all the way. I guess we have had some disastrous happenings to us since our marriage began, perhaps not the exact same happening or occurrences which others have had, but as is always the case, they were not unique problems because they were not unique problems to God or to mankind, we just "colored" them differently.

There was a time when we decided we just couldn't live together any longer. It occurred after the heat of one of those arguments that takes several days to culminate and several more to get over. Bob put most of his clean clothes in the car and left. He must have gone at least to the corner before he turned around and came back. He pouted for days. It was not as if he were coming back to me but coming back to punish me. I don't even remember what started this argument, but I do remember the things I am putting to pen. Misery never knew its company — my heart just knew he felt that he had only enough feeling for me to reach to the first joint of his little finger. I don't even remember who unpacked his clothing — me or him. I do remember we slept back to back for awhile and most of the time I was facing that wall "on my side of the bed" I was crying softly. After most of our other arguments we were always face to face, or closely fitted, snuggling, come morning.

Times were hard by today's standards. but then aren't the times always hard when they are measured by yesterday's standards? We did not feel that times were hard. Gradually our standard of living went upward. Wasn't overnight! so we lived not expecting great things or great financial rewards as far as material wealth goes. But we were happy. Bob was the wage-earner and I was the homemaker for approximately seven and one-half years until our younger son was ready for kindergarten. I am very glad that I did not miss out on those times of being able to be home with the boys during their very formative years — the years when children learn more than they do at any other time of their lives, in values and in experiences.

Great expectations and wild dreams of what marriage would be like before our marriage did not fade away, although plans for making the marriage become a story-book romantic adventure did wane with time. However, the struggles did not completely defeat the cause, because the more realistic things began to appear, the more able I was becoming to deal with them.

Wednesday's menu included salmon croquettes, a casserole dish and home-made apple pie; Friday's meal consisted of hamburgers and french fries; and sandwiched in-between were stew and red beans over rice or meat loaf with carrots and potatoes. Traditionally American meals, traditional American marriage . . . so far, so good. Double feature movies for $1.00 a carload at the drive-in movie or television programming centering largely on game shows and talent shows, plus "Desi and Lucy" and "Father Knows Best" provided our only entertainment. My source of friendship outside marriage was to take the boys with me about once every week to visit my friend, Jean. Jean also had boys and our children would enjoy great times playing together while we visited over a cup of coffee. We took turns on the visits, one week at her home, the next at mine. Jean probably had as much to do with my becoming a Christian as my mother-in-law, whom I loved dearly and from whom I tried to acquire characteristics of disposition. She was as lovely as she was beautiful, as lively as she was gracious, whatever the occasion called for — she was. Up until the last two years of my mother-in-law's life I don't ever recall her showing weaknesses and I suppose she did then because she was laboring in so much pain most of the time. She was a faithful Christian and helped me as did my own mother in becoming the person I am today.

Mothers-in-law are objects of ridicule, which is unfair, as they can be a good influence. My mother-in-law influenced me greatly as she was a person who appeared to always be in control of her life, and commanded situations with humility. Doing this is an art and few people ever acquire this wisdom unless they walk with God. Very few people can accept the wisdom of others at face value unless they, too, also walk with God and "Have weathered the storms of life."

Marriages do not have to be perfect in order for two people to live together in a working happy relationship. Good marriage partners are raised, in godly homes, where the child is given responsibility and taught to last when the going gets tough. You make a start when you get married, you finish the course when you die. If you feel you are not equipped to finish the race, then don't start, because it will be tough enough in the world where the growing trend has been acceptance of trial and error relationships built upon a set of values which God never intended that man should have. Falling in love is a growing feeling; not an accidental one.

In summary, to be a good mate, one must be cooperative, kind, happy and well-adjusted, have religious faith, and be committed to God. That mate should be willing to leave his father and mother and place emphasis on his/her formed relationship. As it states in Genesis 2:23-25: "Bone of my bones, flesh of my flesh: Therefore shall a man leave his mother and father and cleave unto his wife and they shall be one flesh . . ."

THE MEANING OF TRUE LOVE

It is sharing and caring,
Giving and forgiving,
Loving and being loved,
Walking hand in hand,
Talking heart to heart,
Seeing through each other's eyes,
Laughing together,
Weeping together,
Praying together,
And always trusting
And believing
And thanking God
For each other . . .
For love that is shared
    is a beautiful thing—
It enriches the soul
    and makes the heart sing!

—*Helen Steiner Rice*

Chapter I

Study Questions

1. What are the problems or challenges which can effect a good marriage? Discuss.

2. Why is the scripture Philippians 4:6 important in decision-making?

3. Arguments generally generate from how *we* feel about how things affect *us*. What quality of a Christian will help through overcoming this inadequacy?

4. The following scriptures all teach us to be longsuffering or patient. Romans 12:12; 2:4; 1 Corinthians 13:4, 2 Corinthians 6:6; Colossians 3:12; James 5:11. Look them up and discuss each one.

5. (a) Why are the young lacking in the quality of patience?
   (b) What does the Bible tell us about youth and impatience in both the Old and New Testament?
   (c) Would you perceive that perhaps this might be one reason why the very young have a difficult time making a marriage work? Why or why not?
   (d) Simple occurrences can cause great distrubances and disagreements if patience is not present or learned. The author cited some minor occurrences. Can you name one which affected you marriage in this manner?

6. What is another trait which is common in the young married couples lives which can be detrimental to a healthy relationship?
   (a) What can be done to overcome this trait?
   (b) Why is a sense of humor necessary in situations of learning and growth?

7. Discuss the key elements in making your marriage work?

8. Realism replaces romanticism as time goes on in marriage and this is a good trend to allow one acceptance of things as they are.
   (a) How did you come to grips with what became real in your life when the honeymoon was over?
   (b) Would you find it helpful to find a role model (a person who

15

could provide inspiration for you) as you adjust to the new problems you incur when you begin to find out you and your husband are two different people?

(c) Can you still afford to be a little romantic in some things?

9. Do we *fall in love* or do we *grow in love?* Explain.

10. Name some of the traits necessary to becoming a good mate.
   (a) With God, all things are possible. Can we develop these traits even though we have not learned them during our lifetimes?
   (b) Can you name other traits which you feel help make a marriage work?

11. Can one still look to his father and mother to help him/her with decisions and learn to be a good marriage partner? Wherein should the limits be placed in our dealings with our parents? (Genesis 2:23-25).

[1]*20th Century Christian*, July, 1981, p. 9.

[2]Helen Steiner Rice, "The Meaning of True Love," *The Greatest Of These is Love*, compiled by Donald T. Kauffman is used by permission.

Chapter II

IN STAYING IN LOVE WITH MATE

Staying in love. Ah, that's a challenge. I suppose everyone, even those who appear most devoted, feel a type of hatred for their mate at one time or another. The fleshly part of us generates emotion akin to hatred when we become extremely angry and become defensive because of that anger. I would rather never feel this emotion called hate, but I would be lying if I said I could completely contain it, although I know that as I have become more spiritual and been given more wisdom, I have been able to control and have power over my emotions. The feeling which I initially termed hatred was one that came and went, as an emotional fire triggered mainly by desperation and frustration, but it never lasted long, and as I began to understand myself better and feel more comfortable with who I was and what God expected of me as compared to what I expected of myself, the bitterness affiliated with the hatred did not linger in my mind or dictate actions I should take. I learned a technique whereby I realized my impatience with others and learned how to step back, take a good look at the situation, and determine what God would have me do. When I really became angry at my mate, this strong image of his strength would always appear to me and I melted into him as one once more. It was as if I could feel his strength as well as gentleness and the lure of his childish nature to the soles of my feet. He could be across the room from me and if our eyes met, his eyes alone told me that I was still the bride he married and that I always would be. Men's memories probably don't serve them as romantically as do women's memories, but then women are geared for remembering things like tender moments

17

which stick like glue in their minds. They may forget all else — but never a tender moment.

Although many people use Matthew 19 as a scripture for not staying together, the scripture certainly is misused by these people because this scripture presents what Jesus gave as being reasons to stay together. Nothing can make love sour as bitterness in the heart. Colossians 3:19 states "husbands love your wives and be not bitter against them." This should be for the wives, likewise. Indifference is a tragic component in the breaking of a marriage.

Research has indicated that many marriages become happier as years of marriage increase. According to studies conducted by Dr.Robert Lauer, Dean of United States International University School of Human Behavior, "men and women in happy marriages tended to say that the most important ingredient of their union was that they basically liked their spouse." The spouses were described as "their best friend" and they confessed they liked "them as a person" and that the underlying respect and liking of their mate carried them through the rough spots. Lauer's study went on to state that "fair fighting" or focusing on the issue rather than the person; spending of leisure time together, and knowing that marriage is rarely a 50-50 proposition were also important components in making a marriage last.[3]

To stay in love with your mate, you had better be sure that you have picked a mate worthy of every test, because 9 out of every 10 marriages will run through almost all of the tests. These tests will be "colored" differently, but they will be tests of problems akin to problems which others have had. What do you do if you don't have enough money? What do you do if your mate becomes physically unattractive (most of us must confess, with age there will be sags, bags, wrinkles, veins, baldness, stooping, false teeth, etc.)? What if your mate becomes very ill and can no longer fulfill the responsibilities or enjoy living life with a certain degree of normalcy? What do you do if you lose a child? What do you do if your mate is out-of-work? What do you do when children leave home? What do you do if you and your mate's interest vary greatly? There are many important questions in the tests. If you allow yourself to grow together through a mutual period of courtship and to continue that growth with marriage, you will be equipped mentally and emotionally, as well as physically, to deal with most of the problems.

God rations out the calamities in our lives. This week it will be one thing; next month it will be another and next year there will be a "biggie"! He won't give you more than you can bear as He promised that.

I have stayed in love with my mate by first getting someone I really liked as a person as well as someone who was physically attractive to me, and then practicing! I practiced until I hurt! "Practice makes perfect" — the old cliche works. I practiced holding my temper; keeping my mouth shut; biting my tongue; silence; laughing. Did I practice! You know what? He was practicing, too, but it takes men a little longer to perfect practice techniques. They have to be reminded with subtle hints of important days coming up (like anniversaries, birthdays, etc.) as well as reminded of those things which really annoy you.

Positive things were also in the practice schedule. Occasional smiles were practiced; being around him when I could see that he wanted me there, and doing the little things which I saw made him happy were also practiced. One should not practice anything that causes resentment to build up during the practice period. Above all, practice listening — truly listening to the verbal as well as body language. I practiced hard, I was committed to a cause — making my marriage work, and I know that he wanted that too, because he was practicing, and we kept getting better at things as time went on, and now we are so aware of each other that our thoughts often appear to merge as one.

If you don't practice staying in love with your mate through all the seasons of life, then you had better practice losing him; perhaps not in the physical sense of his moving out of your life, but in the sense that only his skeleton remains, and his mind and spirit are elsewhere. He may remain faithful and you may, too, but it won't be an enjoyable or pleasant relationship. Mutual understanding and communications occur when there is a meeting of two minds and a commitment with the desire of communicating harmoniously. You may be under the same roof, but when the children leave home you will be two strangers.

A question was asked in a People Quiz of *Family Weekly* magazine as to whether certain qualities were more significant for the wife. The findings were cited as follows:

1. The significant woman actually represented very powerful influence on the man.

2. One of the ways in which this influence is characteristically manifested is its ability to change him and lead him to different types of experience, especially to an expanded awareness . . . of emotionality and spirituality; and

19

3. The significant woman possesses the potential to fill in or counteract gaps or weaknesses that the mate perceives in his own personality.

I have a method which I have tried to tell younger women to use which revives and rekindles my interest or makes me more aware when I feel I am losing these characteristics of awareness of my husband and his needs. It goes like this. Watch your mate — just stand back and watch him when he's tinkering with the car trying his best to repair it, or when he becomes totally involved with a project. He's neither helpless nor victorious; he is oblivious to the world around him — totally absorbed. Study him carefully. Try to close your eyes and meditate on the young man you married; he's still there — think hard. Fall back into memories of what he was, why you fell in love with him and your strong feelings for him at that time will become strong feelings again. Open your eyes and I can promise you, you will love him, with grease to his elbows or whatever, you will love him. The same procedure works well anytime he is doing something in which he appears to be totally absorbed — e.g., riding that horse he loves, walking in the woods when you know how in tune with nature is his heart, or watching his favorite comedies on Saturday morning (yes, men love them!), or any other one of a number of observable portions of the man's world. After doing this observing, I am always compelled to go to my mate and kiss him gently and say, "I love you," and then just let it drop at that. He's always surprised, but always pleased. He never fails to note my reaction because it's always unpretentious and unpredictable and appears to make a lasting impression. You know what it is? Appreciation — just appreciation, that's all, for him, for his just being him. This is unspoken communication, vibrations . . . but he picks up on my interest in him as *a person and not just a thing;* I share my house with things and objects; I share my feelings with *him.*

I continue to appreciate my handsome husband and to owe an eternal gratitude to the man my husband's parents made — just for me! As Hannah dedicated her child to God, a dutiful, beautiful, God-fearing Christian mother-in-law and father-in-law dedicated my mate to God. I will do my part to see that I never misconstrue that dedication and service to God.

Chapter II

Study Questions

1. Can we feel emotion like hate and still be Christians and loving mates?

2. Christ became angry in the temple and "sinned not". Can wives become angry with their mates and not sin?

3. Read Matthew 19. Is this scripture misunderstood often? Why? What do you think Matthew meant or implied about staying together in marriage?

4. Colossians 3:19 speaks of bitterness of husbands.
   (a) Does this not also imply wives bitterness?
   (b) Can you name some synonyms for bitterness?
   (c) What is the command spoken of here?

5. How can couples "fight fair"?

6. What are some "tests" of marriages?
   (a) With what can you meet these tests?
   (b) Does God ever stop testing? Explain your answer.

7. The old cliche "Practice makes Perfect" can pay off in marriage. At what things can you practice to make your marriage work better.

8. How important is it that marriage partners learn to 'read' body language of their mates? Could this ability serve to ease bad relations, as well as know when to 'ease off' or 'fill in'?

9. What are two traits necessary for a committment in marriage?

10. Are some qualities more significant in a marriage? What are some of these qualities? Discuss them.

11. Can you think of a technique which you can use effectively which will rekindle a tired, faltering flame, loss of interest, for your mate?

12. Can unspoken communication aid a marriage? How? What are some 'unspoken communicures' you can use?

13. Can we realize a commitment to God at the same time we realize a commitment to our husbands? How? What does Paul say about the relationship of wife to husband, wife to Christ and His church?

14. Truly there is an art in the showing of appreciation. Godly women can show this appreciation. How?

[3]Editorial, *Modern Secretary*, November, 1984, p. 9.

[4]People Quiz, *Family Weekly*, February 22, 1981.

A question was asked in a People Quiz of *Family Weekly* magazine as to whether certain qualities were more significant for the wife. The findings were cited as follows:

1. The significant woman actually represented very powerful influence on the man.

2. One of the ways in which this influence is characteristically manifested is its ability to change him and lead him to different types of experience, especially to an expanded awareness . . . of emotionality and spirituality; and

3. The significant woman possesses the potential to fill in or counteract gaps or weaknesses that the mate perceives in his own personality.[4]

The *20th Century Christian* magazine submitted a plan for strength which the writer felt very appropriate for entry into this work. In order for the couple to meet the challenges during the first three years of married life, the couple should:[1]

1. Spend time together and become truly acquainted.

2. Recognize the marriage as being their marriage.

3. Face problems as money management, sexual problems, whether to have children as directly and optimistically as possible.

Chapter III

IN DOING AND NOT WORRYING

Did you know that time spent in worry limits active time in doing a job? Sure you did! Then don't do it — the worrying — I mean. I want to share with you my finally learning to worry less and use my energies in positive ways. Now mind you — I still have not learned to totally escape worry. But when I find myself slipping back into the old ways of worry, I spend more time in prayer and conditioning my mind to think on positive things in life.

I learned how to worry very well — practice makes perfect and did I practice. I practiced how to practice worrying. Worries for me centered on whether the sun was going to shine so that I could hang out my wash, and I had a dryer; whether or not my clothes were hanging in the right order in the closet so that I could match them as I rushed about early every morning. Sounds very foolish, but we are all guilty of this — trying to handle our own problems with no consideration of the fact that we need not bother, because we have help with our problems all the while, right at our "beck and call" — God is always there.

My sister-in-law had suffered from a breakdown and my precious mother-in-law had gone to get her and take care of her while she tried hard to piece her life back together. The strain on my mother-in-law was tremendous. She could never leave her alone for even a little while over one and a half years. When our family went to visit, we could feel the pressure and found it difficult to even make the visits. As my mother-in-law became less able to deal physically with the problem, I worried about how I would take care of my sister-in-law when my mother-in-law passed away from the strain and stress. I needn't have worried; my sister-in-law died of a coronary while sitting up in a chair one night.

My mother-in-law was an independent's independent. She was vibrant, attractive and very likeable, and one who enjoyed her lifestyle and wanted no other, but her health was failing more, coupled with the fact that she was over 80. However, she had been climbing mountain nature trails and fig trees up through her 79th year. She was always tempted to climb the loose limbs of a large fig tree, making the remark that the best canning figs were always at the top of the tree. A description of her physical agility would be to say that she was a 50 - 80 year old. I worried about how we would be able to contain her in our household and let me run my household normally and still keep her happy. I needn't have worried about this, because she slipped away from us only seeing one of those precious to her standing at the foot of the hospital bed, who was telling her "Come on — Mamaw, you're a fighter, give it your best try!" His pleas were in vain as they buzzed for a code blue, and told him he would have to leave the room. She had suffered a massive coronary a year after the death of my sister-in-law.

God knew all of this. See how futile all the things we worry over are. The pieces of my life and the manner in which God directs these pieces to fall into place one by one seems so very simple when one looks back. But we cannot be futuristic as to seeing what God has in mind for us, we can only know that there is nothing under the sun to be apprehensive and worrisome over, because all things, whether they appear to be bad for us or good for us, "work together for good to them who love the Lord."

For goodness sake! Do something about whatever troubles you, don't continue in a worrisome vein. The doing begins with a supplication or thought of turning that problem over to God. When you set the thoughts in motion that problems are no longer *your* problems, but those which have become problems you share with God, then there is a transference that takes place. As a psychology major, I learned many years ago that transference was one of the techniques that works so well allowing one to handle his/her problems. Don't tell me that one cannot use this technique and have it work when that one is dealing with a power so great that the Almighty One, God, who literally spoke the world into existence, cannot handle a little transference from several million people at once. Have you ever stopped to realize how many people God must be "listening"(our term, not His) to at once? If he listened as we do, with His ears, He would be limited.

Can you just imagine the awesomeness of His listening power. As my students would say, "Man, that's mind-boggling!" I said all this to say one small thing — turn your worries over to God. He knows all, He already has knowledge of your decisions, whatever they may be, before you make them; but, if you ask His direction and His will, He can help you go the right way — which will eventually mark the pathway to Heaven.

Scriptures on Anxiety (worry):

"Be careful for nothing; but in every thing by prayer and supplication with thanksgiving let your request be made known unto God. And the peace of God which passeth all understanding shall keep your hearts and minds through Christ Jesus" (Philippians 4:6,7).

"Cast all your care upon him; for he careth for you" (1 Peter 5:7).

"And having food and raiment, let us be therewith content" (1 Timothy 6:8).

Luke 12:22-31: Jesus spoke to His disciples and told them to consider:

" the ravens: for they neither sow nor reap; which have neither storehouse nor barn and God feedeth them: how much more are ye better than the fowls?" (verse 24).

"And which of you with taking thought can add to his stature one cubit? (over a foot — tip of finger to elbow) (verse 25).

"Consider the lilies how they grow; they toil not, they spin not and yet I say unto you, that Solomon in all his glory was not arrayed like one of these . . ." (verse 27).

Chapter III

Study Questions

1. Can we afford to be futuristically looking forward to plans without considering God?
   (a) Does this not lead to more worry if we do without considering God in our plans?
   (b) How will considering God's will make things easier?
2. What methods can be used to lessen worry? Discuss these.
3. Form groups of 4-5 to talk about worry.
   (a) Each group member list 5-10 things she has worried about during the last 2-hour period.
   (b) Each member reads list.
   (c) Others can decide which they consider most important.
   (d) Others decide means of solving worry for other group members.
4. Some scriptures dealing with worry to help you and lessen the stress and strain caused by it are: Matthew 6:19-34. Read and discuss these scriptures.
5. Is energy expended when we worry which could be used elsewhere?

Chapter IV

IN MATTERS OF RAISING CHILDREN

Rearing children is probably the toughest job anyone could have and certainly is one of the most responsible jobs. Parents generally find that most of their children are different. When people make the remarks, "My, you certainly are like your father or your mother" parents will assume that this is complimentary and they want their children to pick up on their values, mannerisms, and appearances. Children are imitators. Naturally, children are around parents more than all others — surely they would tend to copy them. Remember the story of the male child being left on the prairie and being raised by wolves. He acted like a wolf; he was not able to talk; he made the sounds he heard the wolves make; he could not walk upright; he ate like a wolf, and if he cleansed himself, he did so like a wolf. The wolf boy did not know that he was a human being, having never been around humans, so he imitated the wolves of the pack. The wolves did not know he was human — he smelled like them; he acted like them.

The lesson in this is that parents need to live the lessons and values that they teach and want their children to follow. This is also a good reason why only responsible adults who can be good examples, should be allowed to care for your children while you, as natural parents, are away from them. Generally, parents tend to think in terms of safety for their children, but they should also think in terms of the children's well-being.

Children need both parents very much, but if such is the case where the children have only one parent, then a father/mother substitute should be given consideration (whichever the case, missing father or missing mother). The mother substitute can be someone the teen-age girl can go with problems as she begins to mature and cannot understand the changes going on within her body chemistry. Her father may not be able to fulfill this need for a substitue mother when the natural mother is not around. The son who has no father around may feel a real need for that father when he begins to test his limits of disobedience to a mother who may be unable to contain him. In my family, I often found that my husband spoke a language which the boys understood much better than the correction which I was providing. Sons without fathers often become resentful, hateful, and possibly develop psychological problems — I truly feel that sons need a male model around with whom they can identify. Having not had daughters, I am limited in my knowledge of first-hand experience as to how the daughters compensate. However, I was one of three daughters and do know that my mother generally provided most of my correction, as well as that of my sisters.

Certainly more time and space needs to be given this problem than has been provided. As a matter of fact, a whole book could not contain information on any of the problems encountered in raising children. The versatility of problems incurred by parents could never be called simple and could never call for simple solutions in all cases; nor could any two problems with nearly same symptoms be handled exactly the same way because the problems are occurring to people with different personalities. I know you noticed that God did not make any two of us alike — except maybe identical twins, and although their personalities tend to be more alike than all other's personalities, they are still different. One "pat" answer cannot be given, unless the "pat" answer is that the solution of all problems in dealing with our children must be solved with God as a Offeror of solutions (prayerfully solved).

Parents must never live their lives for their children but live their lives for God, so that when the time comes they will be able to let go. God did not intend for the bird that has left its nest to fly back to that nest again. Watch the habits of the Purple Martins. Even though they spread the word to return to their old homes each spring, those martins that come are new martins, building new nests, but in the same houses provided by humans for them. The Martins have strange life patterns and we would be wise to study them. When your children leave home will you have a life of your own? Have you been building a relationship with your mate so that you can dwell in your house together, in oneness, and not as two separate individuals with no common ground? As hard as you may try, you cannot salvage your children from the pitfalls and dangers which they will encounter making lives for themselves, you can only bring them along to that point whereby they will be able to act responsibly and keep God in their lives so that He can take them onward and upward.

We hinder our children in "Making It" when we try to help them make decisions or make their decisions for them when they reach maturity. We should instill the values that will equip them for proper decisions so that when they are called upon to make decisions, they do not become emotional cripples when they are finally told, "Now, it is completely up to you." Granted there are many things we do not let them decide upon while they are maturing, as going to the dentist, attending church services, getting their homework, sometimes going to school, etc. Most children, I am fearful, would decide against doing any of these just mentioned. However, if guided, and not controlled, if neither being lax or domineering, if criticism is balanced with love, and character is shaped and molded properly in order that trust is instilled, then the child can handle his resources, talents, and skills. The child must be taught to live to make the world a better place for all and not just for himself; to be humble when he is victorious; to be courageous when he is defeated, to look at the faults of others and know that the faults he sees are his faults, so that he will not be judgmental; to be taught to hear and see with his heart and soul. Only through these teachings can the child direct and control his life. As that child walks through his life into adulthood, through the seasons, from spring into winter, he will have left some of himself along the pathway and others will know that he is still with them when he has departed. So, you see, parents who really love their children, will never lose them completely, for parts of the children's lives will belong to them forever, and the part that they could retain, if they did not follow God's directive and let them go, they would not be happy with if allowed to do so.

When we make our mark on the world then we have fulfilled our mission for having been. Our mark may be through the lives of our children, and this is why we need Godly parenting.

Rudyard Kipling's poem, "If" is so expressive of how I feel about teaching children how to grow.

If

If you can keep your head
when all about you

are losing theirs
and blaming it on you;

If you can trust yourself
when all men doubt you
and make allowance
for their doubting, to;

If you can wait and never tire of waiting
or being lied about, don't deal in lies;
or, being hated, don't give way to hating;
and yet don't look too good, nor talk too wise;

If you can dream
and not make dreams your master;

If you can think,
and not make thoughts your aim;

If you can meet
with triumph and disaster,
and treat those two imposters
just the same;

If you can bear to hear
the truth you have spoken
twisted by knaves
to make a trap of fools,

or watch the things
you gave your life to, broken,
and stoop, and bend them up
with worn-out tools;

If you can make one heap
of all your winnning
and risk it on one turn
of pitch-and-toss,

and lose, and start again
at your beginnings
and never breathe a word
about your loss,

If you can force your heart
and nerve and sinew
To serve your turn
long after they are gone,

and so hold on
when there is nothing in you
Except the Will

which says to them: "Hold on!"

If you can talk with crowds
and keep your virtue,
or walk with kings —
nor lose the common touch —

If neither fores nor loving friends can hurt you,
If all men count with you —
but none too much;

If you can fail
the unforgiving meet
with 60 seconds
worth of distance run

Yours is the earth
and everything that is in it
and — which is more —
You'll be a Man, my son! [5]

The proper rearing of children is probably the most complex job anyone is ever given. There are no simple solutions to most of the problems that parents have in getting their children reared. But one thing for sure, it is a difficult task and anyone who attempts to do it without God will not "make it" successfully. 1 John 4:1-4 says that little children are "of God." Matthew 18:3 states that the childhood stage is very important to God — "Except as ye become as little children." John teaches us to be like children, and his teachings of the innocence and purity of children is a clean, pure state, without sin (1 John 3:4).

This places an awesome responsibility upon parents — they have children come to them by being the natural parents or adoptive parents and these children are gifts from God, truly pure and innocent. Do we corrupt them? Does the world corrupt them? Who should bear the brunt of the blame when a child goes wrong? Parents — society? If we follow the scriptures and "bring up the child in the nurture and admonition of the Lord" (Ephesians 6:4) then we will have seen to it that we have done what we could and not have guilt feelings about what we could have done and did not do. Of course, the parent must follow all of the scriptures in so doing, so that he/she becomes the parent God would have him/her to be. This includes gentleness, kindness, meekness, and all the other characteristics which so ably describe a Christian.

Parenting is a difficult task for both husband and wife, or father and mother. Disagreements over the rearing of the children in a family is a source of conflict, particularly if we do not do it according to God's word. Joseph thought his children were "the sons whom God had given him" (Genesis 48). And Solomon also felt that children were a gift from God when he said, ". . . Children are a gift from the Lord: the fruit of the womb is a reward. Like arrows in the hands of a warrior, so are the children" (Psalm 127).

Children need role models to identify with as Paul writes in Ephesians 5:1 that our children are to copy God. The power lies in the example that we set for our children. Children need to be taught diligently as is found in Deuteronomy 6:7. Parents should search for teachable moments.

A gradual sharing of problems can help children be conditioned so that when they grow up and face similar problems in their marriages, they will be able to handle them. Children need to understand that when an expense comes up as tires for the car or repairwork, then there may not be enough money for that special dress or shoes. The techniques and principles we use in families to relate to each other are the techniques and principles they will use when they grow up and relate to their mates. Families need to relate deeply and meaningfully all their lives together and when the children mature, they will relate deeply and meaningfully. Parents help their children face facts instead of shielding or protecting them.

Teach your children that they are special — so special that they should think more of themselves than to smoke pot, take drugs, commit illicit sex, drink, or otherwise abuse their bodies.

Every parent wants to be perfect. We are not; we must be realistic and when we find ourselves in crisis times as our children grow older, we question our own values; then comes the time when we can be friends with our offspring, and they become friends with one another.

Don't ever fail to leave the molding to God, just provide the proper clay and He will shape the design.

As mates who find that they indeed get along together and want their children to do likewise when they choose a mate, we know that since we are able to love that our parents must have loved us. It is so important that parents properly love their children and these children also will love and be able to give their children love. We should teach our children of their worth as human beings and creations of God, and that life is very important. We should also teach them that it may be easier to follow our impulses, but that we should follow truth. In these teachings we will also teach them that they must be able to live with themselves now and in eternity (Ecclesiastes 12:13,14).

If we have done the job as we should, acting maturely and as Christians in raising our children, then we know that we have furnished our generation, the next generation, and generations to come with those who can keep the world on the right course (see 2 Timothy 2:2) ". . . commit thou to faithful men, who shall be able to teach others also."

Married partners who have children will find their proper relationship to their children which should be done according to God's will, will serve twofold purpose. The proper relationship developed by making sure that our children develop intellectually, "advancing in wisdom physically, in stature," and spiritually, in favor with God; and socially, "and man" (according to Luke 2:52, 1 Peter 2:21), will make our homes a secure, safe, good/stable environment for both ourselves and our children. Our children will learn how important life is, especially the good life; they will be "copers" and will, in turn, help us cope better.

This one important statement I leave with you "on raising children." Through the eyes of my children I catch the reflection of what I have been and what I am.

Chapter IV

Study Questions

1. How is proper child-rearing associated with the making of a better marriage relationship? Discuss from the standpoint of how it affects the family/husband/wife relationships and (2) how it affects the making and molding of a better mate for another.

2. Parents should not only be aware of the safety of their children when they are in the care of others, but of values they may be learning.
   (a) Cite examples of how we teach our relationships with others.
   (b) Is it important that a single parent teach respect and admiration for the missing gender in the family?
   (c) How can this be accomplished?

3. What is the only answer for finding correct solutions to problems incurred in raising children?

4. How can parents help their children make good decisions and live within them?

5. What does decision-making have to do with commitment?

6. The child you raise is the adult who will either live to earn the respect of others or fail and possibly blame his parents for his failure. Do you agree or disagree with this statement? Explain your answer.

7. Explain the term "Daddy parenting."

8. Read 1 John 4:1-4. Children are "of God." Explain this.

9. Matthew 18:3 states the importance of children in God's eyes. Certainly all parents see the relevance of this. Apart from needing children to be so there could be adults, why did Jesus teach of their significance?

10. Ephesians 6:4 speaks of how we must raise children. What are these directions? Discuss how you are going about this responsibility.

11. What characteristics make you a better parent?

12. Reread Genesis 48 and Psalm 127. Joseph and Solomon felt attached to God through their children. What did Solomon mean when he compared children to arrows in hands of warriors?

13. Do you have to set your children down in a similar to school sitting to teach them? What are teachable moments?

14. What does loving your children have to do with their becoming loving mates?

15. Reread Ecclesiastes 12:13-14. Discuss.

16. Reread 2 Timothy 2:2. Discuss.

17. Reread Luke 2:52; 1 Peter 2:21 for the scriptures on raising children.

18. Good marriage partners are coping people. How does study of the Bible and following the teaching therein make people more able to cope as their life progresses?

19. Do you understand my poetic statement "through the eyes of children I catch the reflection of what I have been and what I am"?

[5]Kipling, Rudyard *"If"* *The Home Book of Verse*, Ed, Henry Holt and Company, 1945, 7th Edition.

Chapter V

MAKING IT
IN FINANCIAL MATTERS

Financial matters are always a source of problems for the majority of people most all of the time, so why should financial problems be any the less a problem for married couples. Unless one happens to live in a country where bartering is done, and then I suppose bartering would pose problems if one had little or nothing to barter with.

To be financially bankrupt is terrible, but to be spiritually bankrupt is devastating. Challenges can be met if you have the attitude that you can do all things through God. Some families set up special plans and run their households accordingly. We have families whom I know in which the man of the house does all of the marketing, clothes shopping, paying of bills, and gives the wife an allowance; and those in which the woman of the house takes upon herself all these responsibilities. Whatever works for these couples is fine. If these situations do not create problems for those in them, then they should not create problems with our accepting this type of plan. In our family we have bounced the responsibility around until we found one which worked best, with the least amount of frustrations for all. For awhile my husband did all of the bookkeeping and I was glad for him to do it because, although I was a Business major in college, I was the one with the least amount of spare time for performing the tasks as he was in college and I was working. Later on, he continued to have the time while working shift work and I was at home busy with the children and at the same time working on my master's degree, so he continued to do the bookwork. However, when he went back to finish his degree and start teaching and coaching, he had no time, and I took on the job. Today, he is happy with my book work and leaves all of the financial management up to me, but he does keep track of things and we always talk over any type of financial arrangement that affects both of us and our relationship and our future.

Most times money problems arise out of a couples' desire to have more 'things' than they have money. Most families with adequate budgeting can sustain themselves quite well, but when our eyes "become larger than our pocketbooks", we initiate a series of problems that will come upon us one after the other and if left to continue, will dissolve even the best relationships. It goes like this. We own a $30,000 home, but we want to purchase one in a better section of town which is selling for $75,000. So, we sell and we go into debt for a balance which we cannot hope to pay off, not in our lifetimes, at interest rates of 15% or more. Because of the high notes on the new mortgage, our home notes take up three-fourths of our income. Impossible, you say — no, possible, but everything else must suffer. We then find that we are slaves to a thing, a house. Pressure builds up and we find that we cannot give to the Lord, we cannot take a much needed trip for a rest or time away from our everyday lives, we cannot even find $200 to attend a Christian workshop.

The answer to the aforementioned problem is to be realistic: keep your lifestyle as simple as it can be kept. Spend your money on the important things in life and do not let American commercialism brainwash you into thinking that all the material possessions advertised will bring you happiness.

I guess I am like Thoreau in that I am attracted to the call of the woods. My husband is also. We find that one of our most pleasurable experiences is to go to a beautiful camp grounds in Arkansas, set up a tent, cook on a Coleman stove or grill, play 42 with friends by a Coleman lantern and listen to a camper far away in the bush strum on an old guitar. Camping never cost us much money, and it may have been a little rough as far as comforts go from time to time, but our memories of camping are as some of the happiest memories of our lifetimes that we always enjoy sharing from time to time.

The home which we possibly enjoyed the most was one which we created ourselves from a house that looked as though it belonged to a set on the movie of "Ma and Pa Kettle." My husband and I enjoy a private joke about a picture which hangs in our den. It is an enlarged photo of a ramshackled old house built at the turn of the century, dilapidated and looking as though it had shared its fame with many families for many, many years. When people came into our den to visit they always stare at the picture. My husband tells them that is the "Before" picture of our house. He quickly reiterates, confesses to his story, but *never* before he feels like they are completely captivated and awed by the amazing recovery the house has made. The walls are decorated with old plow shares, tools, decoupaged pictures, and handcrafted items, which we found,' cleaned, painted or redid. The bedspreads are home-made quilts fashioned by either myself or my very talented mother-in-law. All the decorative glass pieces were crafted by my mother-in-law. There are so few items that have actually been purchased from stores at any cost to my family that I could count them on my fingers. Even most of the furniture is restored from pieces no one else in the family would have. So, you see, what makes people happy does not necessarily have to be expensive or like that which the "Jones" down the street have.

This extends to the children of the family also. That which costs the most is not necessarily what they desire. A denim sports jacket made from faded blue jeans was one of my oldest sons favorite pieces of clothing.

Because of the responsibility of managing my own earnings since the age of 14, a responsibility I am glad was given to me by my parents, I have always been able to spend wisely and save industriously. Investments of what were very small amounts at one time, grew and allowed us some of the luxuries of life (a new car when the old one wore out; home improvements when the house was in dire need of repair; travel money for vacations once a year). As my husband has never been a spender, and one who would even be comfortable in his old clothing forever, money for personal belongings never became a problem, either. However, whoever manages the pocketbook, or the checkbook, should never close it so tight that he/she loses site of certain needs of individuals which are affordable and which can be necessary.

For a man to know and believe that he is able to take care of his family has always been important to the head of the household. Some men will accept help from outside the immediate family circle more readily than other men. To have to appeal to others for money to make expenses is degrading and an insult to others. Some 'men' depend wholly on outside help because of lack of management of family finances. These men receive their paycheck, if they have one, and spend it before they set aside for necessities. If these men marry women of that same inclination, then there will be trouble very soon after they marry. Of course, marriage counselors can help them, but the couple should have dated long enough to realize that they both had a very important inadequacy which would tend to make their marriage relationship difficult because arguments would ensue just because of debts, creditors cannot wait for people to pay at their convenience. Often the problem of being unable to manage personal finances causes loss of employment. My experience in working in a large industrial company and handling garnishments taught me much on how financial mismanagement can hurt the people involved.

If two people really want to make it and consider themselves "spendthrifts", it can come in the form of classes in accounting, business mathematics, family finances or family budgeting courses offered at vocational schools (often these courses are free except for textbooks and papers), high schools, churches, and colleges.

It was my unfortunate knowledge to once be acquainted with a head of a household who was just the opposite of what I have described. He held onto the purse so tightly that his family and his wife, especially, began devising dishonest ways to get a dollar or two for herself once in awhile. Every penny had to be accounted for. He paid the bills; he bought the groceries, household items, clothing; he carried the children to the barber shops (both boys and girls); he wrote all the checks and doled out exact change to each member of the family for every item of expenditure. He was the lord and master in all things, and yet he was not a hateful man. However, he was never generous either. The family was a captive and they appeared and acted as captives, and being around them made others uncomfortable. Was this the type of plan God had in mind? No. This marriage was in as much trouble as the first example presented. The thing that troubled me most about this relationship was, "What about the death of the master of the house?" How would the family manage; Would the quiet, subordinated family be able to function in the world and manage to survive, or would they just go out and spend every cent because they finally could spend without question?

Then there are families like ours. Either partner could do the financial management efficiently, and although neither was preoccupied with extreme thriftiness, values determined where money should be spent and how much money should be spent. There was always enough money put aside for a set of new tires when the old tires became slick; but there never would be enough for a Hawaiian vacation. We had always been an average-income family, understood what that meant, and lived on the average-income with a national economy paying no heed to what our average income could purchase. Cost of living rose, taxes went up, prices went up, and salaries stayed the same; with products being built to live shorter lives. However, we

40

shifted money from "this to that" and from "that to this" in our family budget and we accepted and dealt with the problems as they came up. Clothing was worn longer, fashion "be-hanged", hamburger was deliciously prepared, haircuts took place at home, repairs were made instead of purchasing new items, air-conditioners were turned up to 80 and heat down to 68, and we slipped down into the middle of our tipping economic canoe and "rode smoothly down the river with the tide." And you know what was always so great? We *always* had enough.

Why did we always have enough money? No one else ever does these days. However, they really do — if they are with God. In 1 Corinthians 10:1-3, "collection for the saints . . . let each one of you put aside and save." We had God in mind first. We had practiced purposeful giving to God's work and this always came first from our earnings *before taxes.* What started out as 10 percent because we felt this was what we should purpose, not because New Testament scripture says this is the amount we should give, we have been able to move upward since that beginning. As we expanded our giving, we became more able to give.

Every time that our family was faced with economic crisis situations, we came through. A check would arrive in the mail — not an inheritance or one from a long lost relative, but a refund check, or we would be able to earn a little extra or cash in a policy. If I had kept a journal on how many times God has answered my prayers on matters of this nature, I would fill several pages with information on exactly how the prayers were answered. Getting children grown doesn't lighten the load much, I remember when we were trying to figure out how we were to fund our son's wedding, without sacrificing our retirement savings. Don't let anyone tell you that a young man's wedding expenses are not much in a large wedding. They are — especially if the young man married a young woman in another state and the wedding is very formal. Well, the year before the termites had eaten away the framework of the "L" part of our large dining room, which we had condensed and repaired at considerable personal expense, but for which we had been unable to collect on our termite insurance policy. To make a long story short, we had waited, talked, written and waited some more for the company to reimburse us for the basics; the company refused, so having taught a business law class, I wondered if we might not be able to collect legally. We did, and half of the damages were reimbursed and we used this money for some of the wedding expenses. The rest went on the "magic card" and were paid for monthly.

Saving and planning in accordance with earnings is a key to

financial management. Discontinuance of credit buying as much as possible, except for large purchases as automobiles or furniture, which can hardly be afforded any other way. Use a budget which is adjusted to earnings. Investments should be made wisely and with advice of those who know about such things. Sometimes parents can be a great deal of help here because they have made wise investments. Never let money cause you to go away from the truth (1 Timothy 6:9-10).

The key to our "making it" financially was not in my ability to divide a dime, but in God's will for our lives. We planned that He should come first. First, even when a new car was needed or even when a large medical expense demanded large payments. First meant first — God got His share of a total which was truly *all* His, and we never faced a need which was not met. We would have felt the pangs of guilt had we not given God His share. Sometimes, when I look back, I am still awed by His ability to smooth out the wrinkles in the rough of a budget and yet be the provider of so much for us. His goodness overwhelms me.

People sometimes feel that those who are wealthy, materially, are very fortunate, but having had several members of our family who were financially well-off, and being in closer association with these family members, I found that they have some of the same expenses and problems as most of us. They just drive larger automobiles, live in larger houses, and dress more expensively.

Many people say, excusing themselves, "Well, we had some medical expenses this month and we couldn't get very much together for giving." One can always make excuses for mismanagement for the Lord's funds. Some people value new expensive automobiles, lavishly-furnished homes, but cannot seem to get around to place more than a few dollars in the collection plate so that God's work can go forward, as is written in 1 Corinthians 16:2, "upon the first day of the week let every one of you lay by him in store, as God hath prospered him, that there be no gatherings when I come."

There are those who do not give as prospered on purpose, because these people disagree with some of the financial plans of the church. Churches have planned missions, meetings, and aid for missionaries, orphans, and many programs and unless the elders know approximate funds in advance in order to conduct the programs, they must cancel them.

Financial matters and associations and transactions are controversial with many marriage partners, but I believe you will find that by the time the majority of couples live the major parts of their lives together, working at living harmoniously, you will find that financial matters which were controversial at one time are no longer sources of disagreement. Compromising, learning to take turns giving, becomes the order of the day, and compromising is a key to communication and problem solving. Some call this wisdom.

A married couple should never procrastinate on doing something about putting their financial affairs in order, because to refrain from doing so robs them of time which should be used doing other things with your family and for the Lord.

Matthew 6:19-24: "Lay not up for yourselves treasures upon earth, where moth and rust does corrupt, and where thieves break through and steal: (20) But lay up for yourselves treasures in heaven, where neither moth nor rust doth corrupt, and where thieves do not break through nor steal: (21) for where your treasure is, there will your heart be also. (22) The light of the body is the eye: if therefore thine eye be single, the whole body shall be full of light, (23) but if thine eye be evil, thy whole body shall be full of darkness. If therefore the light that is in thee be darkness, how great is that darkness! (24) No man can serve two masters: for either he will hate the one, and love the other or else he will hold to the one, and despise the other. Ye cannot serve God and mammon" (KJV).

Chapter V

Study Questions

1. Is there one method for managing finances which works more effectively than all others?

2. Are there financial matters which are considered relevant to both partners which should never be dismissed without consultation with both partners?

3. Why do you think financial matters become such serious detriments to a happy marriage?

4. The Bible teaches us realistical simplicity in a lifestyle. Can you cite examples from the Bible where this is taught? Discuss.

5. Reread 1 Corinthians 10:1-3. These passages speak of collection for saints and putting aside.
   (a) Why is it important to give to the church and needy causes?
   (b) What is meant by purposeful giving?
   (c) Is saving for our old age important? Why or why not?

6. Read 1 Timothy 6:9-10. Can money cause you to go away from the truth? What should you do about this?

7. In 1 Corinthians 16:2 Paul spoke of laying by in store as you have been prospered so you won't have to rush around at the last minute trying to make restitution. This teaches more than giving to God — it teaches us to avoid this type of spending and living so we are not "stuck" without having alms for what is the most just thing (returning to God what is His). Discuss the scriptures mention of "1st day of the week . . ."

8. Do our financial needs change as we enter different 'seasons' of our lives? How?

9. Matthew 6:19-24 tells the believer how to deal with treasures and what is most important in life. Discuss the 22nd verse. (eye-singleness-light) Discuss the 24th verse. (masters-love and hate)

10. Wherein do we find our greatest reward when we are able to give liberally and joyfully?

11. Cite examples of how you felt when you were able to give a loved one a prize gift with no selfishness.

12. How many times have you purchased a gift for someone because it is something you would love to have and it gives you so much pleasure to give it as a gift? Why do you suppose you felt this way? Why was it so easy and joyful to part with the gift?

Chapter VI

IN PLAYING THE PROPER ROLE
AS A WIFE IN SEXUAL MATTERS

To be a wife means that I must be a helpmate to my husband, a lover, a friend, a person who stays at his side through sickness and health, through adversity, and unhappiness, through sorrow and pain, until death separates us in the physical form we now have. Spiritually, a strong, courageous mate will never be separate from the other mate. Thoughtfully, the mate stays with them forever. I can think of nothing else that gives me any greater joy than knowing that not only will I share Heaven with God, Jesus, Paul, Noami and Ruth, and countless others, but that I will share Heaven with my earthly mate, my best friend, and one who deserves the highest form of love which I could give him while I walked this earth and shared his life.

I have always been afraid of telling how real and effectual my feelings were toward my husband when I would listen to women talk or complain about how unreal and ineffectual their feelings were toward their husbands. Maybe it was because I was afraid that they would think that I had the remarkable man worthy of their taking; that he had something that most men did not have. But, now I see and understand that what we have together, no one can take from us. Building a bond, or lasting relationship does not come from the joining of any two persons, male and female, but from trust, faith, concern, giving and taking. Given my husband, another woman may not have ever made a marriage with him last; given me, another man may not have ever made that marriage work. We can learn from other's experiences, but we can never be the same as those persons or have exactly the same experiences, even though we know that "there is nothing new under the sun" (Ecclesiastes 1:9).

God determined that "it was not good that man should be alone," and He made a helper (Genesis 2:18) for man. Now, I know that God knew exactly what He was doing. God also intended that a son or daughter leave their father and mother and become "one" and that no one should come between man and his wife (Matthew 19:4-6). He also intended that they should give to one another conjugal rights 1 Corinthians 7:3-5), and that the "marriage bed be undefiled (Hebrews 13:4). God also stated that we should feel no anxiety (Philippians 4:6-7), and this includes the fact that we should have no anxiety about loving our husband as we love ourselves. Thereby, I will have the type of relationship with my husband which God intended that I should have.

Sex is an important part of a total relationship in marriage. One should not have guilt feelings about enjoying sex with her mate. In fact, we owe it to ourselves to be worthy of the term God used to describe it — "becoming one." There is a sense of pleasure like no other in this oneness.

Before sex relations can be satisfying, emotional and spiritual qualities must be "in tune" or made right. Sex should not become just a fulfillment of a flesh, or bodily urge. It is very important that there be no guilt or sinful feelings in the sex life of you and your husband. Guilt feelings can arise from so many things which we have done which have collected in our subconscious mind and God did not need Sigmund Freud to come out with theories about this. We don't even know the limits of our minds and how the mind of man controls actions, but God did, and He knew that if we hang onto dead memories without seeking forgiveness that the old "ghosts" would affect full concentration and involvement on whatever we were finding to do in the present. He brought this out when we are scolded for carrying "around the dead man of sin."

The Bible gives examples of how we are to overcome guilt by using the story of Adam and Eve in Genesis 3; by studying of David in 2 Samuel 11 and 12, and Psalm 51, where David prays for forgiveness; in the lives of Peter and also of Judas, in telling how differently each of these men handled their guilt, in Matthew 27:3-5, and Luke 22:54-62.

Guilt time reflects that we are thinking only of self; so what we need to do is learn from mistakes and get busy with our present lives. In Philippians 3:13,14 we learn how Paul handled this guilt.

Coitus is the ultimate physical expression of love in a husband and wife relationship and neither partner should ever let their love get to the point where sex becomes a mechanical happening. Sex should remain the beautiful, expressive, thrilling experience which God thought was good. I am always amazed at how lightly, we, as Christians, tread over the scriptures where God made Eve for Adam. We capitalize on the sin that evolved, instead of God's intention that here He had done something really "Good." He didn't intend that Adam just stand around and stare at Eve — they knew what each other could do for the other. No matter how hard the world takes a beautiful thing and reduces it to a thing of depravity, as coitus; the act itself could have come from no other source than from God.

Sex has been given an ugly description by writers, by television, by movies, by abased thinking, Satanically inspired, in the minds of men, and that is a pity, for the coming together of two persons, male and female, is so very beautiful. Beautiful is one of only a dozen proper words which would describe the conjugal blending of two into one.

I can remember my husband's reaching for my hand during courtship days and how just the touch of his hand on mine would send tremors up my spine, and I recall those moments we had after our marriage when we had so many gloriously happy times in the building of an intimate relationship that could always pull us together when we seemed to be on the edge of despair in other realms of our lives. When everything else appeared to crumble around us, and we had one another and could still share our oneness in the sexual realm, it was as though we were lost to the other problems which surrounded us, as we perfected our oneness in this sharing.

We get so busy with our lives that we don't take time to enjoy one of the most gratifying, uplifting, natural events that God designed our bodies for — and that event is in making love that is removed from guilt in the sanctity of a bond between a male and female, in marriage. Climb the tallest mountain to take in the beauty of what lies thousands of feet below; rise to the height of truest of all true feelings and emotion to human feeling: the mating of man and woman, in God, and according to His will, delivers a feeling like no other. No matter how old a man and his wife get during the term of their marriage, they can find a delightful meeting of the minds and converging of the flesh and soul in making love with one another.

Today there is much clinical and scientific knowledge about sexuality and although it has been thought of for many years that men lose their ability to perform the sex act as they become older and that women never had any interest in it from the beginning, this falsehood has been found to be totally without factual backing. It is strange how people accent the worldly rendition of most viewpoints. Just the other day, I was discussing the age of some of the men of the Old Testament. The school teacher with whom I had been discussing the matter commented, "Oh, time was accounted for differently in those days." It would have taken longer than the 5-minute break to reteach the error of this woman's thinking, but I did try to set her thoughts on the right track and give her a reference. Men *were* that old in Biblical times! And according to studies in genealogy of the Bible, they did not lose their prowess in performing sexually because of their great age. And the older women weren't standing around. Sara had Isaac when she was 90. I just cannot believe in Abraham's day that the women were hiding from these Biblical men or telling them that they had a headache.

Impotence of men is not a natural part of the aging process and can indicate physical diseases, disabilities, and psychological problems. Treatment is available for all of these problems and should never be avoided if treatment can keep an otherwise healthy relationship going.

Personally, I feel that as women get older they become more interested in perfecting their sexual relationship with their husbands and that they feel better about intimacies and certainly much more comfortable with them than they felt when the house was bulging with children, chores, and there were fewer "chances."

A willingness to experiment and a wonderful sense of humor which comes with age, lack of embarrassment at most things which would have put one on a guilt trip years before, brings the married husband and wife to always feel the agape love first and the physical love which comes from the total sharing of the agape love, second.

If telling the world what the world says is love is not love, and that what the world sees as sex in the pairing of "partners", not married mates, is not spiritually fulfilling, and telling them instead that true lasting happiness comes from building a type of relationship in which there is total commitment and responsibility, and that will, in turn, result in a blending of two lives into one, and caring feeling which supersedes all others — agape love, then this good news should be shouted from the housetops. People should never live and then die and leave others to believe that there was no in-between in their lives. The in-between was the secret of finding true romance and the in-between was total commitment.

The more I studied God's plan for marriage and what I have gotten from my marriage, and wanted my children to get from theirs, should they decide to marry, I became more determined that some way, either by talking with them, or writing it down for them to read, that I would share some of the intimacies of their father and I with them.

What? How could you do such a thing? Why, that is totally against human nature. You should never share those things with anybody. And to that I am telling you, if I had a daughter, I would share them with her, and knowing the trust which I have in my sons, I know that they will never share the secrets of their father and I with the world. Who could benefit the greatest from my having shared what I feel is so tender, so awe-inspiring, so lovely, so good. I want them to be the man their father was when he was at his best and know that as or- dinary as we may ever have seemed to them as parents, we were always extraordinary in our lives with one another. That things have been as good in the past for those who have gone before us as they can be in the future, and that "there is nothing new under the sun." And with this thought, I painstakingly sat down and wrote a five-page let- ter to my youngest son on a tender scene between a young man and his bride and I knew that he would know that it was of his father and me that I wrote, because I told him this was true and that as hard as he may have ever found his father to be, he was the most gentle man I would ever know, and that he, too, would do well to learn from his father's gentleness from a part he may have never been able to see had I not granted him insight.

Married couples from the beginning of time certainly enjoyed the blissful moments found in sexual relationships. There are no new ways to make love; what has been tried or will be tried is not new and those who write exposes on the art of love-making are telling the same old story in different sentence structures. Thousands of people spend millions of dollars searching for truth in feelings which God gave man a natural ability to feel, but which will be impossible for man, if man does not return to the point of true spirituality.

All of us know that in order for things to be all right in the sexual realm of our lives, things must be all right with us. It goes back to reading and studying the Bible and learning how the Bible can affect our lives, turn them around, and make us complete. Only then can we make others in our lives feel complete about themselves.

Wives should practice sensitivity to your husband's feelings — key in and be perceptive to him and try to understand action instead of the personality behind the action. Read the vibes. Gear your conversation and watch the body language. Many times even an outsider can observe and know whether a married couple are in physical harmony, so surely it is possible for the wife to be able to judge her mates actions when necessary.

Married couples do not need to blunder through their lives

accepting mediocrity in sex or perhaps never experiencing true climactic pleasure. A thing worth doing is worth doing right! Please don't ask me "How's to do right?" Right is not what is right for just you, but right for both you and your mate, and when you find it, you will not need me, as a layperson, or any type of expert tell you how, or to impose upon you feeling of guilt, inadequacy, or frustration.

Another thing worthy of mention: I do not like to use the negative, but will in this case. Don't play "shut-out" all day long and play "close quarters" at night, or whenever you happen to be alone. Daytime conversations, day-time sharing and concern will put you on the stairway for a "night-time plateau." If he decides to come give you a fond pinch when you are up to your elbows in soap suds washing the dishes, don't shake him off — you were appealing to him as he watched you and at that moment he wanted to be close to you. Share a little soap suds on the towel and a little on his neck and turn and give him that special kiss. I still love the pinches.

Looking forward to sharing with my husband was one of the things that always put me in the mood to love him completely. Maybe it was just a little statement, "Let me share this with you," or, "did you think that I handled the situation right?", "perhaps you can offer me a suggestion . . ." I was so grateful for his confidence and I felt so very close to him at those times. He is so strong, but he needed me! The one who is needed is so very fortunate. All of my married life, I kept saying to myself, "Isn't this the greatest, here is this big, strong, vivacious man who could very well do most things with little or no help, who has always needed me and he let me know it! How much more fortunate can a woman be. In his ever-mindful, sometimes bungling, seldom perfected, but never half-way of telling, he managed to always put out the signals at the correct time that he-needed-me; that I was an integral part of his life. Is not that God's formula for love — agape love. And as he served me, I also served him. I always wanted to let him know the same thing, that as I needed God, I needed him.

Couples have different habits to denote closeness. You have heard of a man's special chair for reading and watching television. My husband and I didn't have a chair. We lounge on the sofa, oft times the small one, called the love-seat, together, often holding hands or touching. We often sit close together when we go places and the kids we work with at school love to tease about this one. We still hold hands in a movie, when there is one that has a rating which we can go view. We are "in tune" with one another after having lived together for such a long period of time. We have seen other couples do it, and over the years we have mastered the art of communication without saying a word. The two of us, placed in a room full of people, can send out messages to the other with a tilt of the chin, a peculiar smile, a wink of the eye, a shrug. We "read" each other so much now, that often when one person starts to speak, both start to talk at once using almost identical words about the same subject.

Yes, good and godly husbands and wives know that the true pleasure of sexual relationships can be found in the same qualities which denote Christian personalities — commitment, fidelity, dedication, and consecration to the vows made at the altar when they were enjoined in marriage.

GROWING OLD IN LOVE

I come to find you sleeping quietly.
  Dear, familiar form
  That I have loved so long.
It seems unreal, somehow,
  kneeling here beside your chair.
That such a snowy head is yours
And shoulders droop
From tiredness and from time:
The hand I hold
Is weak, with fragile skin
And spots of age. . .
  Oh, my love,
  Was it so many yesterdays ago
  That youth and strength
  Filled every cell
  And not a hair was white?
I see within this sleeping form
The man of early years
With proud dark head
And flashing eyes.
Infectious smile.
Shoulders strong and broad
To carry all your load
And part of mine, sometimes
And these dear hands
  — I kiss the aging skin —

Were deft, yet gentle still
In work and play and love.
Your step — so feeble now —
Was firm with purpose then.
  Oh, my love,
  How time has flown
  — These years we've lived as one;
  Yet in my heart
  All our goals
  All our working,
  All we've struggled to achieve,
  — The yesterday and now —
  Are tightly bound together
  Just as the youth I knew
  Lives on
  Inside your resting form.

— *Love Poems* by Bettey Burton Choate[6]

Betty Choate expresses so well in her book, *Love Poems,* the depth of love which one can grow to feel for one's mate, after years of living and loving.

[6]Betty Burton Choate, "Growing Old In Love," *Love Poems,* 1985.

Chapter VI

Study Questions

1. Can you apply Ecclesiastes 1:9 to problems of sexual basis incurred when mates relate with one another?

2. Was marriage instituted by God? When? What did He say about men and women at that time?

3. Did God intend that Eve be Adam's wife?

4. Conjugal rights (1 Corinthians 7:3-5) state that men and women who marry must honor sexual rights.
   (a) Did God allow for times when this is not possible?
   (b) Why do you suppose He knew man needed this form of pleasure?
   (c) Do you believe that coitus is allowed married mates for more reason than reproduction?

6. Read Philippians 4:6-7. Does anxiety affect otherwise healthy relationships? How?

7. God allowed man to have more than one wife during OT history, but was this His original intention? What scripture points out God's intention on marriage?

8. What or who gave coitus a degenerate meaning?

9. Do you think that humans react with guilt feelings toward their mates when sexual matters are discussed because of a "Victorian" attitude taught by those who really had no understanding of God's teachings on such matters? How difficult is it for you to speak of your true feelings with your husband?

10. What do guilt feelings have to do with our being able to relate sexually toward our mate?

11. How can we overcome guilt feelings. Refer to Genesis 3; 2 Samuel 11 and 12; Psalm 51; Matthew 27:35; Luke 22:54-62; and Philippians 3:13,14.

12. Many people act as though coitus generated from evil. It came from God. Why do you think people think this? How did the

misassociation take place?

13. How can good physical relationships build upon good mental and spiritual relationships, and vice versa?

14. Dispute the falliacy of coitus being better for men than women.

15. (a) What is agape love? (b) Why is this form of love necessary for full development of sexual relationships in marriage? (c) How does this correlate with a story some women tell "He was good to be with sexually but he was a terrible husband otherwise," or turn this statement around and reason.

16. Why do you think God knew that we could never become half-way involved and realize happiness?

17. Do you feel that the married couples of the past made love differently than those of today?

18. Can you offer encouragement in an ordinary way that will make your husband find it easier to be intimate with you?

19. What is your opinion of women who make it a point to be beautiful in attire and grooming to gain admiration of others, but are "cold fish" when it comes to building close relationships with their husbands? (b) Have you observed any women who exhibit this characteristic with those whom they should be closest with (including their children)?

20. Are you a willing servant of God? of your husband? Relate these two (service to God; service to your husband).

21. What is God's formula for service?

22. What are the qualities which will lead us in being able to find true pleasure?

Chapter VII

IN PLAYING PROPER ROLE
AS A WIFE IN
HEADSHIP — SUBMISSION

In studying the scriptures on headship — submission in Bible Classes from year to year, I always notice how many couples seem to have so much trouble with this scripture, sometimes to my amusement and sometimes to my dismay. The discussions which follow are usually lively ones, so it goes without saying that this is and always will be a subject for debate. However, I am going to disappoint the reader here because my husband and I have never encountered any real problems from the proper interpretation of the scripture referred to in Galatians 3:28 and Ephesians 5:21-22. Our relationship has never been a question of his saying "frog" and my saying "how high?" Somehow, God spared us of this problem, even though we joke about these matters from time to time.

Since we have always looked upon our roles as being individually satisfying and complementary to each other, and since we have spent the majority of our married lives trying to do God's will, these scriptures have caused no disagreements between us. However, it is possible for me to see that when these scriptures are misunderstood, or improperly taught and imposed upon, or taken from context, havoc would be created. Even our worldly counterparts who will own up to nothing else in the Bible as being relevant to their lives, will jump on any man who tries to explain the scripture as God intended it to be explained.

Just the other day, I was reading a newspaper column about a writer who was advising people on how to become married and stay married, when he himself had been through two divorces. Interestingly enough, he stated that both sides — male and female — go into marriage with the idea of fulfilling certain definite roles; the man expects a submissive, home-loving, traditional, conservative woman, in turn, wants stability, security, affection, understanding, and a happy home-life, and when they go into marriage with those expectations that they will live up to them and make the marriage work. The reason why this writer's marriages failed and many others like his included the fact that the partners had left God out of their relationship, or neglected to put their marriage on the right relationship as God has prescribed.

From Paul's teachings Ephesians 5:22, "wives be subject to your husband as to the Lord," subjection is qualified by the words "as to the Lord" and "in everything" or "in the same manner" or "as part of your subection to the Lord."[7]

Subjection is a great characteristic found in any Christian — male or female. When we care to the point of not caring about ourselves first, we reach the state which Christ proposed we should reach to achieve agape love. I have always felt subjective to my husband, perhaps at one time for the wrong reason, before I really learned the scriptures, but I have never felt like I was his slave or he my master, and I have been in a situation when he was my principal and I had to work under him, and you can believe that this would have tested my outer limits, had I not believed in the scriptures and all taught therein.

Mutual sharing of love and responsibility and equal submission one to another is something that the scripture teaches. Subordination, as we are inclined to understand the word, was not what God had in mind when He referred to marriage; subjection to and submission, as we understand, are the words which we should adhere to. The heirarchy which God wills that we live by is not one of who is superior and who is inferior in make up, but a matter of keeping order in the proper perspective.

We should be in subjection to our husbands as we are in subjection to Christ. It is the quality of Christian life that helps us reach the agape love which is the mark of ultimate achievement between husband and wife, and between the Christian and others in the world. Christians should never feel threatened, but inwardly free in their service as they are both bound and released.

A good woman has a price far above rubies. "a good woman is a free woman and subject to none; a good woman is a servant of all and subject to everyone."[8] Further defined, "A Christian woman is most free of all and subject to none; A Christian woman is the most dutiful servant of all and subject to everyone."[9]

Do the scriptures allow for the woman who is trying to be a godly woman but is being led to the limits of exasperation from an ungodly Satanic inspired mate? In 1 Peter 3:1, the Bible states ". . . ye wives, be in subjection to your own husbands, that, if any obey not the word, they also may without the word be won by the conversation of the wives." This scripture gives women the authority to move into the role of assuming responsibility in leading the family when the husbands seek to distort the Christian objectives of the women. It is still possible for these women to be submissive, and serving, but they are also to show actions and behavior which will re-direct unChristianlike actions and behavior of husbands. There are many examples upon which I can draw in this area. As a teacher of young women in the past, I have shared experiences with some of my students who told me how they handled situations in which they were forced, which meant either taking the righteous path, or turning their backs on service to God. Thank God they chose correctly. One young woman related to me how she wanted to attend church services and take her children, but her husband had blocked her efforts. Before succumbing to his wishes, she arranged to go to church without ever having said a harsh word to him, although he cursed her, took the car keys to the family car from her, and spent days pouting about the house, making she and the children "pay" for not following the Bible in their disobedience of the master of the house. Another woman told me of how her husband managed to be gone when she needed the car to attend worship services and also that he ridiculed her without cause when she rendered service to her Lord. She arose, prepared his breakfast, left it on the oven on warm, brought in the paper and sat it next to a full coffee percolator and empty coffee up, cleaned the kitchen, dressed herself and her children and called for one of her fellow Christians to pick her up for church services. She continued to go by securing rides herself from others who were attending church services. When that husband came back and saw what she had done for him, what do you suppose he felt? If Satan hadn't hardened his heart entirely, I'll bet he felt very guilty about his actions. To this day, her husband is still not a Christian, but she still continues to set the example for her family, serve her Lord, and still be a serving wife. Her husband has become considerate of her, even purchased her a car for her use when he was able, occasionally goes to worship with her, and lost his interests in demeaning her efforts to live by Christ's laws.

Women could hold a strange, bewildering power over men, just as men could hold a power over women and I believe that God designed this uniqueness, but the uniqueness should never become the source of a power struggle with the man and wife. It should be used as God intended and then the power will forever hold its mystery and make the one attractive to the other. Unrestrained, misued, or flaunted, the power could become a frightening force for the will of Satan and thereby destroy the marriage relationship and the lives of those who are involved, in work or careers, or in the family life.

The closeness a couple feels in all activity, whether it be related to the family, the job, or the bedroom, uniquely enough is always related to how good each of those partners feels about himself/herself. Things begin at the beginning — so the old saying goes. If we feel all right about ourselves as human beings, then we can relate to others as we should, in whatever we are involved — whether that role be wife, mother, or servant. All the psychiatrists in the world are still in the business of figuring out a prescription to help man dissolve his problems and learn to live productive, active, acceptable lives and the answer on solutions on how to do this are where they have always been — in Christ's teachings in the Bible.

One woman with whom I am acquainted is a perfect example of a completely passive personality. She claims that she and her husband have never disagreed, let alone argue. Not intending to be facetious, I would like to praise this woman because she has reached a hallmark and God has a special place in Heaven for her. I cannot grasp this passiveness in a relationship as being God's will. To live is to contribute; to be passive, is total acceptance, never rising to a level of excitement for a cause, or to love or be open with those we love. Let's face it, all things are not perfect — and to float through life pretending that one is surrounded by perfection is hypocritical. This woman's husband decided everything for his family, and obediently his wife followed his wishes. She had no opportunity for input into anything which concerned both of their welfare or the welfare of their children. For me to allow my husband to be burdened with all the decision-making alone would be unfair and cause him unnecessary stress, burdens, and possible guilt feelings, which would, in turn, perhaps shorten his lifetime. After all, he did not decide that I should marry him — I decided. We have a mutual respect for one another's intelligence, and since we are on a par with like value systems, not too many problems come out of the decisions once they have been made.

Perhaps more information on the wife's role in headship — submission role will be employed in the section on developing the C's of a marriage. What is important is that we remember that Jesus put a high value on women as He performed the first recorded miracle at a woman's request. He took time out for the sinful woman at the well; bragged on Mary and compared Martha's inability to see what was important, and practically with Mary's wisdom; and as He took His last breath He looked down and spoke to John regarding His mother. Women came to His tomb first. I believe that Jesus wants all women to grow into full Christianity and be willing servants to all mankind and through our servitude reach out and try to change attitudes and hearts.

Chapter VII

Study Questions

1. Read Galatians 3:28 and Ephesians 5:21, 22. Determine what is meant by *subjection*.
2. At what age do you reach the agape love intended for Christians?
3. What is meant by subordination? Give an example.
4. Define subjection to Christ and subjection.
5. Explain "A Christian Woman who is free and subject to none, but also dutiful servant of all land subject to everyone."
6. What do the scriptures teach on a woman's position who is being sidetracked in her Christian efforts by an ungodly mate? See 1 Peter 3:1.
7. Has God designed women and men with special holding powers, which if used constructively, can be mesmerizing or tranquilizing?
8. Does the Bible, in Jesus teachings, give the prescription for finding happiness? Where can you find this scripture?
9. Did God intend that women be passive?
10. What value did Jesus place on women? (Check the story of Martha and Mary; what role did women play in their devotion and service to Jesus life?)

[7]Dwight Hervey Small, *Marriage as Equal Partnership*, Grand Rapids, Michigan: Baker Book House, 1980, pp. 57-58.

[8]Martin Luther quote from Elaine Stedman's *A Woman's Worth*, Waco, Texas: Word Books, Inc., 1975, p. 58.

[9]*Ibid*, pg. 89.

Chapter VIII

IN DEVELOPING
THE "C" CHARACTERISTICS
OF MARRIAGE

My husband helps me grow in trust, love, and faith and know who and what I am, and it is my prayer that I also help him grow in trust, love, and faith and know who and what he is. Each of us share equally in the daily struggles of life. However, we do more than this. To this end I have coined terms which I will call the C's of a good marriage, which makes remembering the traits you want to aim for easier. They are: (1) Communication; (2) Commitment; (3) Consideration; (4) Collaboration; (5) Courage; (6) Christians. Because one particular C is a part of each of the other C's — and that C is Christ, if you follow Christ's teachings you will be developing and putting to good use the other C's.

First, good marriage partners are (1) *The Communicators*. After many years of practice, I believe that my mate and I are communicating better than ever. When we first married, we talked, and even tried hard to communicate, but we often failed at it because we were still immature and managed to interpret and perceive only that which we wanted to perceive, which was not necessarily what the mate communicating wanted understood.

Matthew 5:37 states "But let your communication be yea, yea: nay, nay: for whatsoever is more than these cometh of evil." In other words, don't mess around with words! Many times it is best to refrain from saying anything than to say something and it be the wrong thing.

As a public school teacher, I have worked most of my life trying to teach students to communicate properly so that they are not misunderstood. In Luke 24:17 Jesus asked the disciples to communicate with Him and with one another. They were talking to Him but were not aware of who He was, and as soon as they discovered who He was, having not even been able to recognize *Him*, He vanished. Isn't that just like us? As soon as we really know others, they leave us. Think of the time that could be spent communicating unselfishly. In 1 Corinthians 15:33, we are told "Be not deceived; evil communications corrupt good manners." This is pretty self-explanatory. One of the characteristics of any Christian is to practice letting God control our lives and thereby we will communicate wisely the thoughts God would have us say or do.

Ephesians 4:29 declares that one of your Christian duties is to "let no corrupt communication proceed out of your mouth, but that which is good to the use of edifying, that it may minister grace unto the hearers." One cannot get in trouble with his tongue in this manner.

The Committed. Commitment means service. Jesus had a position equal with God in heaven, but He relinquished the position to come to earth and render service, to even abase Himself, even for those who would express hatred for Him, for *All* of mankind. We are to strive to be like Jesus; to role model. "He who is greatest among you shall be a servant," (Matthew 23:11) so, doesn't the wife have a greater glory than all because we are called to serve, we are called to glory!

If either mate fails to live continuously in Christ, the other mate is never free of his/her role to be the mutual servant of that one who has failed him/her. Commitment allows for no escape. Commitment reaches goals—and our goal is heaven.

Commitment counts—numbers don't! I had rather have one committed person on my side than a dozen uncommitted when I have to take a stand for something. Job 5:8-9 reads "I would seek unto God and unto God would I commit my cause: which doeth great things and unsearchable, marvelous things without number."

Paul felt a commitment in that a dispensation of the gospel was committed unto him (1 Corinthians 10:17) and if he did it willingly he would have a reward.

Psalm 31:5 reads "Into thine hand have I committed my spirit: thou has redeemed me, O Lord God of truth." Again in Psalm 31:7, which is called David's Psalm, it states "I will be glad and rejoice in thy mercy: for thou has it known my soul in adversities."

On a 20-20 program recently aired, February, 1985, it was my pleasure to witness several married couples express their views on making marriage work. A famous television newscaster expressed that he had been married 42 years and that he and his wife were interviewed and a statement which he made which was very significant was "marriage took work and that it was worth it." Interestingly enough, the couples who were interviewed felt that statements from a famous psychiatrist indicating that all marriages which lasted very long were due to a compulsive dependency need and not from a higher form of love, were wrong. All interviewees, even one couple married 70 years, felt that their love had deepened spiritually and physically and was more than a dependency relationship, and they stated that they had worked very hard at making sure that their marriage was never ordinary or their relationship was taken for granted, that they felt a deep sense of trust, friendship, and commitment to one another. As the cameraman faded out the scene, he focused on the older couple sitting side by side, and lowered his camera to the arthritic hands reaching for the other mate's hands.

The Considerations. Consideration for one another tops the list of important things to remember. Partners in life grow when they are nurtured in thoughtfulness for one another. After all, most of us treat those with whom we work or deal with outside the family relationships with thoughtfulness and consideration, why not do this with those we love the most.

In Luke 12:27, the Bible states that God has considered the ravens and the care of them, and stressed how much more worthy of His consideration were we. And in Matthew 6:28, "And why take ye thought for raiment? Consider the lilies of the field, how they grow, they toil not, neither do they spin." Isn't this a beautiful passage? Not only does it teach us not to worry, but it teaches us that God's consideration of mankind is that of the highest form of love, agape love, and we must remember that we are to know that when we feel least considered that God has considered us most important of all things. At all times, even when we reach the pits of depravity, He *considers* us.

Just as Paul was inspired to write in Ephesians 4:32: "Be kind to one another, tenderhearted, forgiving each other, even as God also in Christ has forgiven you," he gave the prescription for building a growing loving relationship with your mate. Galatians 5:13 also teaches us to help, serve, edify, build, and encourage. Carefully followed, these scriptures cannot help but lead one to build a relationship that can last through time and tribulations. These are the elements of consideration one for the other.

The Collaborators. To collaborate, to work together in a joint effort, especially intellectually, on dreams. Dreams keep people alive and going forward. Dreams sustain people—when everthing seems to become commonplace, it's much better for a couple to reach for shared dreams than for material possessions. We cannot just keep having and getting. My husband and I have dreamed of a special home for the 31 years of our marriage, and we have had the plans for 25 years, but we have never had the money to build the home, even though it is modest. We just bought old places, remodeled them by ourselves as we accrued the time and the funds, or we rented from others. We have dreamed of travel, of grandchildren, of success in a special job we never were able to obtain, of family fun, of old times and good friends, of service we never took time to render, of beautiful horses and acres of land planted with beautiful rye grass for grazing, of a yardful of flowering dogwoods, of beauty, and lands unseen. Even though our dreams were thought of simply by one of us, these dreams became the dreams for two of us and whether we can ever make them real, we can still share the joy of just having a dream. And in these dreams we came to know one another better, down deep where knowing is so much richer and better.

The Courageous. Courage is steadfastness and strength of character. A person can be courageous on their own, but when two people combine courage, it's awe-inspiring! Combined courage, from two who have become one, metals melted and forged by facing trials and tribulations, frustrations, and heartbreaks, and brick walls and disagreements, all met with courage which came from the bond of two people.

I was raised on a ranch and Daddy was always trying to keep old gates together by using old pieces of metal and when he would send me scurrying off to find an old scrap of metal to use to piece some fallen piece back together and I would come running and say, "Daddy, here's a piece, it's nice and shiny." "Nope," he'd say, "ain't tough enough." Off I would go and come back with an old rusty piece and to that piece, he would reply, "Nope, ain't been used enough, rusty." Exasperated, I would make another trip to the scrap pile where one usually digs up these sorts of things on a ranch and as I ran to him again, holding up my prize, he'd say: "That'll do just fine, see, it's been beat up on, oughta be tough nuff to take it!" Metal that is used, just like a good knife, will meet the test of time; in a sense, we are like metal.

Deuteronomy 31:6: "Be strong and take good courage, firm nor be afraid of them: for the Lord thy God, he that doeth good with thee; he will not fail thee, nor forsake thee."

Psalm 27:14 states "Wait on the Lord: be of good courage; and he shall strengthen thine heart: wait, I say, on the Lord." Psalm 31:24: "Be of good courage and he shall strengthen your heart, all ye that hope in the Lord."

Paul was running for safety and he thanked God and took courage in Acts 28:15.

Perhaps experiences which we have as children give us the courage to face the problems we have as adults, because courage must be learned.

The Christians. Being Christians is the last characteristic mentioned, but by far the most important, for it is in the relationship which we have with God that helps us achieve the relationship we desire in marriage. Christianity has been found by many to be too difficult. However, life itself is difficult; Christianity can only make a difficult life easier.

Paul is one of my favorite Bible personalities and I use him and his life to teach many lessons to my Bible students. Paul's second letter to the Corinthians tells how much he went through (2 Corinthians 11:23-33). Paul's preaching and teaching were dynamic and "all that heard him were amazed" (Acts 9:20), . . ."the Jews took council to kill him" (Acts 9:23), and he went to Jerusalem to join the disciples, "and they were afraid of him." (Acts 9:26). Paul was doing great things and having big problems.

The bad experiences Paul had were much worse than any of those we could have as far as physical and mental persecution goes and yet Paul made up his mind he would endure. In 2 Corinthians, verse 23: "in stripes above measure, prisons more frequent, in deaths oft." In verse 24: Paul stated he had received 5 beatings of 39 stripes; verse 25: three times he was beaten with rods, stoned once, 3 times shipwrecked, robbed, spent a day and night (24 hours) in sea trying to stay alive.' He was stoned once, placed in continued perils, hunger, cold, and naked, had infirmities which pained him greatly, barely escaped with his life in Damascus.

Paul made it through his life until he was killed for being true to God and his mission of seeing that the truth was spread so that all could enjoy relief from the burdens of this life. Paul's writings, if read often enough can encourage, strengthen, and cause you to make up your mind to refrain from wallowing in self-pity, because he knew that God would lead him from a bad experience into an experience with deeper more joyful meaning. He said that he could even "enjoy weakness, suffering, privation, persecutions and difficulties for Christ's sake. For my very weakness makes me strong in him."

67

Chapter VIII

Study Questions

1. What are the C's of a good marriage?

2. What is meant by Matthew's statement in 5:37 "Let your communication be yea, yea: for whatsoever is more than these cometh of evil"?

3. Jesus felt communication was important as He asked His disciples to talk with Him and with one another (Luke 24:17). What was the lesson taught here?

4. What is meant by evil communications? See 1 Corinthians 15:33; Ephesians 4:29.

5. The scripture Matthew 23:11 and Job 5: 8,9; 1 Corinthians 10:17 all speak of committment. Jesus was committed to serve, to complete his mission. How are you committed? To your family, and God?

6. What were some of the considerations God made for us? Each class member should be able to name one without ever overlapping another class member's answer.

7. How can the prescription Paul gave in Ephesians 4:32 help you grow a loving relationship with your mate?

8. What are the elements of *consideration*?

9. Are dreams important?

10. What does courage have to do with marriage?
    Cite some scriptures where Bible personalities depend upon courage.

11. Do we learn courage?

12. Relate *Christianity* to success in marriage.

13. Discuss Paul's tribulations.

14. Were Paul's tribulations any greater or less significant than ours? Could we not endure more than we do?

Chapter IX

IN SAVING THE MARRIAGE
THAT IS FAILING

Nick Stinnett, Ph.D., wrote that marriage could be saved by following these principles:

1. Awareness
2. Working Together Toward Common Goals
3. Create More Joy Experiences
4. Renew your marriage
5. Keep your interest in each other high
6. Avoid extreme fragmentation

The comments made in supporting these six items are that marriage partners should: be aware of one another's needs and feelings; find out those things that give the other mate joy; renew the initial contract by resolving to serve the other in a positive way; keep interest in mate by doing something together and observing one another's mannerisms (keeping that eye contact at an all-time high); and avoid extreme fragmentation, or extreme fatigue from burnout by changing goals and objectives and also, priorities.[10]

Those who find themselves divorced have failed in some or all of these items. If divorced partners look to a second marriage searching to find true happiness and feel that they can make that second marriage work, chances are that they will have some or all of the same problems that they encounterd in their first marriage, if they have not been made aware of what was wrong.

As has been mentioned many times in this book, staying married takes much work. There are times when even Christians begin to think, "What's the use?" We say this because we let Satan affect us when we should be constantly appealing to God for help. Also, we should apply Stinnett's standards, just as we incorporate similar standards in our professions or employment. Application of new standards or principles may mean painful extention of old standards or principles. One of the principles which works for most couples, which I recommend, is not just better time-management, but Time-Management. So few of us give proper consideration to the face that we have our priorities and goals set incorrectly as to what is really important to our happiness and the happiness of those we love. When we do this we follow by allowing ourselves an improper balance of time in which to accomplish the priorities and goals. First, we have to sit down and study and decide what is really important (become aware). Write down the ideas you have. Then we have to decide upon some goals in order to accomplish what we want to do about important situations. In setting the goals, we can write down the experience which gave us most joy and ways to renew our vigor and zest for securing a happy life. In order to keep our interest level high, we then must think of ways and means of maintenance of a healthy, happy relationship. Above all, we don't want to burn ourselves out during the process. If we do, then we have done things all the wrong way and we need to begin again at the beginning, because something is amiss. After all, we have all the time there is, all the time which God gave us, to do the best that we can; we owe it to Him and to those we love that we spend that time wisely in His service.

Qualities in a working relationship, or qualities that see to it that couples stay married are not secrets that those couples cannot divulge, but if you asked them to tell you how they managed to keep a good thing going for so long, they would hardly be able to say, "Well, it was this, or it was that." The qualities are there, and to others viewing the marriage and observing the qualities, they are very definable — they stand out; they radiate.

Marriages which started out as loving relationships could be saved if the partners did some of the following:

1. Tell the mate that he loved through deeds as well as words.

2. Be joyful and proud of the mate.

3. Refuse to be judgmental.

4. Be complimentary.

5. Practice forgiveness.
   View the actions of the person apart from the person. Try to forget the pain the mate appears to have inflicted upon you. Look past the pain and determine if you would truly be better off alone.
6. Trust and truth go hand in hand. Accept the fact that we do not tell the truth at all times, but that if we want a relationship to mature and last, then trust and truth must prevail.
7. Refrain from jealous feelings. When we see the "green-eyed monster" entering into our lives, deal with the emotion before it destroys the relationship. Perhaps you have sung the little song with your Bible school students, "love is something if you give it away, give it away . . . and you'll end up having more." Or, you have heard of the parable of the bird. If you let it go free then it will come back to you, but if you cage it, neither you nor others will its beauty enjoy."
8. Learn to accept one another as you are. Sometimes we don't even want our mate to know all the imperfections we have, the things which we feel are unattractive and so we remain strangers on things which should be shared and in the sharing, would lose the significance we have wrongly given them. This is where the "I'm okay — you're okay" feelings come into play. Acceptance of ourselves, will make us accept others more readily. The only perfect person I know of is someone I can share my life with, but whom I can never be exactly like (and that person is Jesus).

Item 1 has been discussed throughout this work and the statement means exactly what is says — don't make telling others that you love them so hard — just do it. You are able to tell the people with whom you work or relate to in other areas of your life that you appreciate them (I can hear myself saying it right now, "Thank you, I really appreciate that!"); you also tell them what a fine job they do when they perform a task for you. Why should it be so difficult to tell the one to whom you should be the closest that you appreciate them and that you love them?

Remember the key line in the movie about love: "love means never having to say you are sorry." I think people who love one another know when the mate is truly sorry for having done something without having to receive a spoken word or two on it, *but* I also feel that spoken words mean so much more — the effort is expended to denote feelings twice; and in this case, twice as much is twice as nice.

The Bible is so full of scriptures on love that all one would have to do is flip it open and almost all verses would indicate that letting others know that we should love as Christ loves us is *the* most important thing in teaching salvation to any relationship (God and man; wife to husband).

Item 2: Ecclesiastes 7:14 "In the day of prosperity be joyful, but in the day of adversity consider: God also set the one over the other, to the end that man should find nothing after." And in 2 Corinthians 7:4 "Great is my joyfulness of speech toward you, great is my glorying of you: I am filled with my comfort, I am exceeding joyful in all our tribulation." In Colossians 1:11 "Strengthened with all might, according to his glorious power, unto all patience and longsuffering with joyfulness."

I feel very special most of the time; I am rarely ever down, because I live with such a special person. I am not the altogether person you might picture, it's just that I have two special people at my side all the time, on whom I rely, who keep me assured that I can be altogether, even with my faults and shortcomings. These two special attendants are God and Bob. My joy is secure in that I am a Christian who has found joy in that my mate finds joy in my person. He is proud of me and I am proud of him.

Psalms has many scriptures on being joyful. They are Psalm 35:9 "And my soul shall be joyful in the Lord: it shall rejoice in his salvation." Psalm 63:5 "My soul shall be satisfied as with marrow and fatness; and my mouth shall praise thee with joyful lips." Psalm 66:1 "Make a joyful noise unto God, all ye lands." Psalm 81:1 "Sing aloud unto God our strength: make a joyful noise unto God of Jacob." Psalm 95:1 "O Come, let us sing unto the Lord: let us make a joyful noise to the rock of our salvation." Psalm 98:6 "With trumpets and sound of cornet make a joyful noise before the Lord, the King." David was a person who could "bounce back." He knew wherein his joy could be found.

Hebrews 10:34 "For ye had compassion of me in my bonds, and took joyfully the spoiling of your goods, knowing in yourselves that ye have in heaven a better and enduring substance." So, I know that I can remain joyful in my circumstance, because I know that in heaven I will have a better and enduring substance.

Item 3. People generally loathe criticism; people who are practicing Christianity work at taking criticism in the right manner even though the fleshly part of them has to work extra hard at doing so. But it is possible to criticize wisely and truthfully and not be judgmental. Hebrews 12:23 "To the general assembly and church of the firstborn, which are written in heaven, and to God the Judge of all, and to the spirits of just men made perfect." God is to be our judge. In 2 Timothy 4:8 "Henceforth there is laid up for me a crown of righteousness, which the Lord, the righteous judge, shall give me at that day: and not to me only, but unto all them also that love his appearing." God as a crown for me in heaven which He will give to me after He has served as my judge. Luke 12:14 "Jesus said, "Man, who made me a judge or a divider over you?" Jesus did not even judge the woman at the well while the people were trying to judge her. Luke 6:37 "Judge not, and ye shall not be judged: condemn not, and ye shall not be condemned: forgive, and ye shall be forgiven" The promise is repeated again in Matthew 7:1 "Judge not, that he not be judged." Also, in Romans 14:4 "Who art thou that judgest another man's servant? to his own master he standeth or falleth. Yea, he shall be holden up; for God is able to make him stand."

Item 4 provides a clue to some real harmony and adjustment worth the enterprising effort — be complimentary one to another. After all, when two are made into one, they are said to be complete, whole. To finish off a fine product is to complete it. Wives, see to it that you are a complement to the relationship; that you take nothing away from it, but that you add to it.

Item 5. The truth about forgiveness is that God expects us to extend our forgiveness until there are no limits on how many times that we can forgive. Luke 17:3,4 "Take heed to yourselves: if thy brother trespasses against thee, rebuke him; and if he repent, forgive him. (4) And if he trespass against thee 7 times in a day, and 7 times 7 in a day, turn again to thee, saying, I repent; thou shalt forgive him." 2 Corinthians 2:7 states, "So that contrariwise ye ought rather to forgive him, and comfort him, lest perhaps such a one should be swallowed up with overmuch sorrow." There are at least 44 references to the word 'forgiving' in the Bible. Even when our precious Jesus hung from the cross and decided that He would give "up the ghost," He asked His heavenly father to forgive those who had nailed Him to the cross and who had failed to accept His purpose of this earth. Can we do less?

Item 6. David spoke of trust so many times in the Old Testament in Psalms. Psalm 25:2 "O my God, I trust in thee: let me be not ashamed, let not mine enemies triumph over me." Psalm 31:6 "I have hated them that regard lying vanities: but I trust in the Lord." 55:23 "But thou, O God, shalt bring them down into the pit of destruction: bloody and deceitful men shall not live out half their days; but I will trust in thee. 56: 3 "What time I am afraid, I will trust in thee." 143:8 "Cause me to hear thy loving kindness in the morning; for in thee do I trust: cause me to know the way therein I should walk, for I lift up my soul unto thee." 118:8 "It is better to trust in the Lord than to put confidence in man." 144:2 "My goodness, and my fortress. my high tower and my deliverer, my shield, and he in whom I trust; who subdueth my people under me."

The New Testament words on truth remind us that "the word was made flesh (Jesus), and he was full of grace and truth," according to John 1:14. 2 Corinthians 13:8 reminds us that "we do nothing against the truth, but for truth." Ephesians 4:15 exhorts to the unity of the body and that we should "speak the truth in love," and be more like Christ.

Item 7. Many times jealousy is a much stronger problem-maker in marriages during the first few years of marriage than it is as marriages mature in relationships. Some blame this as a lack of caring as much on the part of the married partners, which I don't believe is really the case. I would prefer to believe that most married couples mature beyond this point. However, many people do let the emotion control them all of their lives and only with an about-face and re-direction by letting Christ direct them can they change.

Item 8. Acceptance of a person, good and bad, by letting them see Christ in you and making them want to be more like you, is the manner one should use to bring about a true and lasting change in the person (if a change is what is needed). "Let your light so shine" and pray for the person.

Chapter IX

Study Questions

1. Is is possible to save a marriage that is failing? What avenues of salvation can a couple investigate?

2. Why do the same problems incurred in one marriage generally occur in a second marriage?

3. List some of the principles which may be employed (used) to save a marriage. Discuss each.

4. How can we keep our interest level high in order to maintain a healthy, happy relationship?

5. Does it help those who are having problems to talk with (counsel) couples who have been happily married? What can they offer?

6. What two elements go hand in hand in establishing loving relationship?

7. Relate acceptance of others to acceptance of ourselves.

8. Discuss eight methods to save a relationship?

9. Look up the word "compliment" and "complement" in the dictionary. Discuss meanings. Relate to God's instruction for wives relationships to husbands.

10. David called God his goodness fortress, high tower, deliverer, shield, and that he trusted him. What did each of these things represent to David (eg. David was strong in battle for he killed Giants with God's help, but he believed in his instruments)?

11. What are our instruments of salvation? Relate them to those instruments of David.

12. The image we reflect to others is like a mirror upon our soul. List the traits others can see in us which cause others to know we want to establish loving relationships.

[10]Nick Stinnett, Ph.D., *20th Century Christian*, July, 1981, Vol. 43.

Chapter X

IN TIME WHEN CHILDREN LEAVE HOME

The time when children leave home is a difficult adjustment period for most, if not all, parents. The emptiness and ensuing loneliness suffered from the loss of the offspring does not come as easily for humans as it does for the animal world. Sometimes parents are inclined to weave their lifestyle patterns totally around their children and the interest of their children. These parents will not be developing a fit child, nor will they be a fit mate; or, if both parents are following this pattern, neither will be fit mates to one another when the children leave home. If the two marital partners have grown together through their years of marriage and not become absorbed by their children's interest, then they will still feel a loss, but they will cope, adjust, and move into new interests and be as happy and content with the new challenges in their lives as they were with the challenges and exciting years of child-rearing. Such has been the case in our marriage.

When our younger son went far away to college and his Dad and I drove away from the college, my heart literally ached and my husband had driven only a few minutes out of the college town and we were both sitting in silence and he turned to me and said, "Mama, let's go back and get him." I could see the glassy film covering his eyes and knew that he, too, was at the point of tears. However, when this son returned home to finish his last couple of years at a nearby college, we knew that he was no longer our little boy, but had indeed grown into manhood and needed to make his own way in the world. The pain that comes from your last child leaving the nest is truly very real and leaves the parents empty inside and yes, God is needed to help you handle this emptiness, also.

When the children marry you again feel this emptiness, but you can adjust and cope with that also because you understand that this is God's will. When my younger son was to be married, I wrote this special narrative for him, did some sketches on the corners of a large piece of parchment, printed and framed it for him and his bride, and performed it as a reading with background music at his rehearsal supper. It was my special gift to him and his chosen wife. I wanted her to know that she would become a part of our family and that we would share our love with her just as Naomi had shared her love with Ruth.

AN OLD CAN FULL OF COINS

I stared through a window pane, looking out at the flowers that had begun to bloom along the driveway and tears began to form in my eyes as I tried hard to hold back the memories. My younger son has been gone from home for some time, but he now approaches a momentous step in his life — his marriage. At this time he will follow the commandment of our Lord which reads, "Therefore shall a man leave his father and his mother and shall cleave unto his wife, and they shall be one flesh." This places the finality of the break in the mother-father-son and/or daughter relationship, except for the commitment resulting out of responsibility and love.

Marriage is sharing: There must never be any secrets in marriage — not even the sparing of feelings when adversity comes along (and it will from time to time). There must never be a refusal to let your mate in on what is going on in your world because what might be happening in your world concerns that mate. In this world there is oneness because you are one, you and your other self — your mate. Total and complete sharing, spoken honesty brings forth mutual trust and shared responsibility. Cry together, laugh together, pray together, hope together, and plan for tomorrow together.

The modern world calls this by many names — total dependency, neurosis, loss of self-identity, total absorption of one's personality by another. Not so, God designed the plan: He knew what it took for man and woman to be happy. God took Adam's rib and He made Eve for Adam: Eve was a part of Adam: Adam was a part of Eve. Until Adam and Eve turned their heads to think apart for themselves in things concerning both of their welfare, they were enjoined in paradise in a perfect union.

During your lifetimes in your marriage, you will have to depend upon a perfect trust and faith to carry you through the trials that come about from a union of marriage, into a perfected oneness. Ah, yes, money is the root of evil, as money has destroyed more marriages than any other one thing — caused more disharmony and unhappiness — whether it be from the lack of it or from the abundance of it. So, for your marriage you save. An old can devoid of its original contents becomes the source for a couple's dreams. Don't flaunt the old can, for its contents are sacred. They save the marriage, for inside are little coins, big coins, and several paper bills, and as deep as the coins become as they are added to the old can, deeper still are the reasons behind the saving of the coins. The pains that come with each coin's removal from the old can leaves an indelible impression upon the couple on the meaning for the coins being.

My mate and I, we had our old can; we still do — for that old can is a part of our past that said, "We are *making it* all right, and we *will continue to make it!"*

So now, I will tell you about the making of a marriage and how it ties in with the old can full of coins.

The baby came ill in the middle of the night and began to run a high fever. Why, had it not been for the old can of coins, the hospital would not have given entry to this very special child — this child, like anyone's child, of course — but this child, this child was *our* child, and we would not lose him because we had our old can full of coins. The bill for the emergency room was $62.00. The nervous father emptied the old can he had quickly grabbed as he headed for the car and he counted out the money. The can held $62.37. He handed the $62.00 to the clerk and she admitted the couple with the bundle in the mother's arms. The father slipped the remaining 37 cents back into the old can.

The amount began to grow again and the car threw a rod, but the wages for the past two months had been just enough to pay for the bills, but the old can was still on the shelf and once again, it was removed from its place. The shop would take a down payment on the repairs and there was $21.42 in the old can. So, the father handed the mechanic the $21 to pay the month's charges on the $250 bill and drove the old model car off the lot. Forty-two cents were dropped back into the old can.

June 2nd came around and both of the partners in life wanted something special to celebrate that fourth year of marriage, so together they took the can from the shelf and began to count. The can contained $19.16, and they smiled at one another — just enough for a fast food restaurant and a couple of tickets to that special movie they wanted to see. There were no pennies to return to the old can.

Winter set in and the season was an especially cold one which lasted well into spring. The utility bills had raged on and dug into the excess budget prepared for such calamities. Looking upward, good old faithful old can of coins, still kept high upon the bedroom closet shelf, caught your weary eyes and liberated your worries and kept you afloat.

Spring finally came and the old can was empty. You noticed that your loved one had been crying alot of late, and you couldn't understand, but there *were* no coins in the old can. So, on the way home from work, the brillance of the springtime blooms caught your eye, and you remembered how you picked the wild onions from the neighbor's yard and gave them to someone dear. You stopped the car, gathered an armful of those beautiful pink and white blooms and took them to your bride of yesteryear, the bride who had lost the luster of her beautiful blue eyes, who had gained the wrinkles from the pressure of life. Then you watched her cry, not in unhappiness, but from joy. She took the can from the shelf and shook it to let you see, that her gift could not come from the old can, so she made you that special pie, that had turned from an inedible, underbaked mess to a delightful morsel in taste, and she placed the luster and growth of springtime in the old empty can and sat it upon the cloth, and you both ate and smiled at one another and then your eyes fell to the old can as you reached for one another's hand.

Then the 40's came and passed through your lives and you neared the 50's and the fall. Life seems easier now, but not so much fun. The worries of the family and their well-being never cease, even though you live in an expansive home with a perennial flowering garden. The house is mostly empty now, except for all the things the children have left behind: Old tennis shoes, scrapbooks, and memories. You closed off all the extra rooms, but you can still hear the giggles of happiness in the night as you entertain the ghosts of the past. You will remember the joy of the morning as you awaken.

The day comes when you go to the closet and far back on the shelf, behind all the worn-out baseball caps, flat footballs, and empty jewelry cases, dolls without eyes, and you reach past them, very high — and there it is — the old can that held the coins. You sit back down upon the bed, not bothering to bring with you the spare rolls of coins that were also on the shelf, and for the first time in years, you shake the old can onto the spread that is covered with a faded design of the Dallas Cowboys' Football Team of 1978. The dust drifts gently into the air. You wonder why you spilled the old can's contents onto the spread. Then as habitually as you had poured the coins from the old can, you count them and tears began to form in your eyes. You no longer need the coins from the old can and you wish you did. The new dress and suit purchased last week at exorbitantly high prices do not excite either mate as new garments once did. The new car sitting in the garage always starts when the switch is turned on: The house is big and empty and so lavishly furnished (never knowing the fear the master of the house once had when he prayed that the guests would not fall when the mended chair leg would squeek and rattle under their weight): The copper utensils hang formally from the kitchen hooks and glitter like gold, with their battered old counterparts set far back on the bottom shelf of the kitchen cabinet.

Echoes of the past — the sound of the coins as you drop them one by one, back into the old can — and now you wish you had that special need, the need for those coins in that special old can, that drew you together and made you one, that you have truly now become — just because you saved and shared for that life together. Oh, that special life together and that speical old can full of coins.

1 Timothy 6:10: "For the love of money is the root of all evil . . . pierced themselves through with many sorrows."

My husband and I are comfortable with our lifestyle, our friends, our professions, and our work for our Lord and our time together. This period is often labeled the "autumn of a seasonal lifetime," the period just before winter sets in, and just as autumn is a gracious, colorful, peaceful season of the year, the autumn of a lifetime can be a gracious, colorful and peaceful time of a lifetime. After all, some people are never able to see this period, so those of us who do, we should enjoy it to the fullest for it is a grand time when priorities change and when one can truly serve Christ and find the time to expand talents he never knew that he had.

The time with our children passes so very fast and is truly not the majority time period of peoples' lives, unless these people have very large families, spread out over a long period of years. Since this period is only a fraction of a lifetime, as people are living longer today, then couples should never let themselves slip into a pit from which they cannot ascend — that pit being forever the smother parents — doting over their children, living out *their* dreams through their children, and never truly letting the children go. They not only do themselves a disservice, but damage the child's ability to make his or her own way and live his or her life.

I have had more than one friend say to me, "I just let Bill or Jim (the husband) go his own way and do his own thing; I have *my children.*"

I always resist the urge to criticize this statement in an ungracious, untactful manner, but if given a few minutes to reply, I ask, "and what will you do when you no longer have your children?"

These women, possibily since the birth of that first child, have sought refuge in their children after having shut their mates out of their lives or had their mates shut them out of their lives. Sad — for either partner to be shut out, knowing this is what is happening, but yet never being able to stop the spiraling trend that will eventually trap them into much unhappiness. It's caused by lack of vision and perception. It doesn't take long in the presence of a couple who have let their lives go in separate directions to pick up on the "rift." This is probably the reason there are so many separations and divorces for couples reaching the time in their lives when their children leave home. The children may have been the only interests that they shared.

The only answer I can see to this problem is to start right at the beginning and head in the right direction and try to stay on the pathway of having the agape love which God intended that mates should have. If you do find that you are headed for problems in this area, try to make some remedial changes that will be effective. Talk to God daily that He will help you change the patterns you are setting and help you start on a road to reinforcement of some new values and/or priorities. Show appreciation to your mate for his/her help or encouragement; put the kids to bed at a certain time so that you have some time off to yourselves occasionally for recreation; to be with people your ages for an evening once in a while; do something special for that mate, (this something special cannot be limited to one description, because something special encompasses a very minute thing to a very impressive thing). The mate generally knows that his/her mate would consider as "something special." It might be a cake he loves; or special lighting for her dressing table; or just some help in cleaning out a closet or storage.

Chapter X

Study Questions

1. We spend the majority of our lifetimes raising children. T or F

2. Why do you suppose we feel that a majority of life's years are donated to child-raising?

3. What does the term "let go and let God" have to do with accepting the periods (referred to as persons) of our life?

4. Can we initiate a gradual separation from our husbands at the birth of our children? How?

5. What can be done to avoid this pitfall?

6. List some ways you have found that worked to rejuvenate your interest in your mate as a person.

7. Discuss times when you feared you were slipping into a pattern of putting other things first and your husband last. How long did it go on before you did something about it?

Chapter XI

IN TIME WHEN ILLNESS STRIKES A LOVED ONE

When illness strikes one mate and the other mate remains healthy, the illness of the one can have a degenerating effect on the relationship, if allowed to. First, the couple must go through a period of disbelief and frightening experiences, or shock, because most of us, even when old, we do not think we will ever be sick or even that we will die. Thank God that we don't live in dread of this natural occurrence, because age does bring about lack of strength and natural immunities, and disease can run its course and do a fairly good job of interfering with life style.

When the period of waiting and praying for the mate's improvement either happening or not happening is over, then comes a period of acceptance, or being able to deal with the adversities of the illness. Finally, there is the succumbing or eventual giving-up to death.

Not only the increasing medical costs are problematic, but the coping in dealing with the effect of chemicals (or medications) upon the body are also difficult to be handled. Medication itself can cause mental distress, anxiety and depression, which in turn, can cause a good relationship to go sour. Medical people often fail to warn the victims of a disease that they may also become victims of the medication they must take and tell them how to cope with the chemical imbalance which occurs within their own bodies. Thank goodness I have a fine doctor who takes much time in helping people by taking time to listen and help out in matters like this.

As much burden can fall on the unhealthy party to come to grips with the reality of his/her illness as the burden which falls on the mate who is healthy to accept the condition of the unhealthy mate. Paul was strong and made stronger by so many adversities. As Paul made it, so can we.

One can only be so untiringly patient, so giving, and so patient without the help of God. Considering that the ailing partner is not abusive, either mentally or physically, or taking advantage of his/her illness as a crutch, most marriage partners are able to deal with illness when they have grown old together. But I have heard it too often that younger people often find themselves unable to deal with their mate's illness and so they flee — they run away. What they don't realize at the time of the running, is that they will have to also live with the guilt of desertion for the rest of their lives when facing the issue with God would have been much better for them as well as the ill mate.

"I just cannot go on, I have been put upon too much!" said the mate whose husband had cancer. See the whittling away? "In sickness or in health," . . . "sure, that's easy enough to say, but try to live it!" the mate went on.

This mate had forgotten the vows of commitment. Commitment takes prayer, much prayer and much extra strength through that prayer in order to continue to be able to deal with the complexities that come into the lives of those who live with those who have become ill.

A friend named Kate said, "It was terrible — month after month watching the strong person I married go down, down, until he was but a skelton held together by small sinews and thin pale skin. You feel so badly and so hurt that you even catch yourself saying, "Why doesn't the Lord just take him, or why me, Lord."

These are perfectly natural thoughts. All people experience them who have watched their beloved mates dwindle down to the depths of desperation in a fight against a long illness. And yet, we still know and believe that God will not give us any more than we can bear. Through all of this suffering, is He not preparing us for something greater, far beyond our present comprehension, that life is not the end; that death is not the end. We occupy life for but a minute time on this earth — we will occupy life for eternity in Heaven.

Some answer this by saying, "But I like this life, I like this body, and I love the pleasures I get from living. I don't want to die. I don't want to give all of this up."

My answer to that, "And what are you really giving up? When there is something greater to be received by the giving, what's to lose?

Those around you whom you love and who love you will be the ones giving up — they will be giving you up. But time and God will heal this. And they will be happy that they gave you up to something so great that they know one day they can be rejoined with you."

Loneliness takes over for a few months after the one whom you had loved and lived with for so long, dies. At first, there is shock, then adjustment, and you find yourself still talking the the second and third person and realize that there is no second person. You walk into a room and you feel his/her presence, and yet he's not there, you want to go somewhere, but you hurry home because he/she will be waiting. It takes a long time to turn loose. Some people never do. Hold on to the memories, but turn loose, so that you can be productive for God. A strong dependent relationship may never be dissolved — but with prayer, you life can still be rich and fulfilling. Work helps. Flowers, gardening, painting, writing; just remembering the good times helps one overcome a loss. Meditating over all that's past will not be helpful. As Jesus said in Matthew 8:22 "Let the dead bury the dead." An old saying, "Idle hands fit the devil's workshop," is also a fitting description of what can happen in our lives when we withdraw from all else. Acceptance of the fact that your loved one can no longer be at your side is a tough step to take but it must be taken for a healthy, useful, functioning, productive life to continue. God does not want any of His servants to "slumber and sleep" through so much of their lives that they fail to do His will. Go on with your life; hold on to the precious memories by rejoicing that you have them, but forever go forward!

A family's presence cannot erase the inward pain and emptiness one feels upon the loss of a loved one, but it helps to have them near and also to have close friends to comfort you, but even if you have no one around at the particular time of a loss, and some people do not (although I have never seen many people who are Christians say they did not have someone with them at a time like this), it must be remembered that you can have no greater friend than God. For I can "do all things through Christ who strengtheneth me!" (Philippians 4:13).

Do an indepth study of Job and his trials; his sores, the pain, and his losses. Even his body was covered with worms and dust (Job 17:1:7:5) and he smelled foul. I cannot imagine anyone going through all that Job did and still be able to keep the faith, but we have God's promise: "Fear not, therefore, ye are of more value than many sparrows" (Matthew 10:29-31).

Chapter XI

Study Questions

1. Define commitment.
2. In what did God promise us our load would be bearable?
3. What stages must a person go through before he realizes he can cope with illness?
4. Those who are not Christians must go through these stages. T or F.
   Those who are Christians do not go through these stages. T or F.
5. Recite the commandment Jesus gave us in Matthew 8:22. Interpret this scripture.
6. Read Philippians 3:13. Where in is our strength supplied?
7. (A) Recall a death of a close member of your genetic family; or Christian family. (B) Discuss the feelings you actually experienced. (C) Did you feel hate for them because they had left you? (D) Did you feel a sharp pain in your chest? (E) Did you feel relief? (F) Did you go into shock?
8. (A) Do you feel fear is one of your worst enemies? Why or why not? (B) When did you lose a loved one? (C) What can be done to overcome your fear?

Calm Repose
or
Grow Old With Me

Grow old along with me.
The best is yet to be.
The last of life for which the first was made;
Our times are in His hand.

Who saith "A whole I planned,
youth shows but half; trust God; see all,
nor be afraid."[9]

Robert Browning

This poem is a favorite of our world for it expresses deep love in prose. I took the original poem from an original edition, with crumbling pages and leather backing, and also secured permission from Random House to reprint it. You will notice that time has given it two titles. After all these years, love as a subject for poetry is still favored, and all the changes in our modern world cannot remove love from being a favored subject 100 years from now.

[9]Robert Louis Stevenson, *An Evening Prayer*, New York: Barse and Hopkins, Publishers, 1895.

Chapter XII

IN HURTING LESS
AND LOVING MORE

1 Corinthians 13

1. Though I speak with the tongue of men and angels, and have not charity (love), I am become a sounding brass or a tinkling cymbal.

2. And though I have the gift of prophecy, and understand all mysteries, and all knowledge; and though I have all faith, so that I could remove mountains, and have not charity (love), I am nothing.

3. And though I bestow all my goods to feed the poor, and though I give my body to be burned and have not charity (love), it profiteth me nothing.

4. Charity suffereth long, and is kind; charity envieth not; charity vaunteth not itself, is not puffed up.

5. Doth not behave itself unseemly, seeketh not her own, is not easily provoked, thinketh no evil;

6. Rejoiceth not in iniquity, but rejoiceth in the truth.

7. Beareth all things, believeth all things, hopeth all things, endureth all things.

8. Charity never faileth: but whether there be prophecies, they shall fail; whether there be tongues, they shall cease; whether there be

knowledge, it shall vanish away.

9. For we know in part, and we prophesy in part.

10. But when that which is perfect is come, then that which is in part shall be done away.

We are eloquent; we are unique, because we are of God. If I am not of God and have not His love in my heart, I am an empty vessel and just as you hear the wind cause the noisemaker to make its noise in the wind, that is all it is — a noise made only by the wind for no sound do I make on my own, showing love.

We can have great knowledge of books because of study and understand 'some' of the mysteries which puzzle others, and have faith, but if we do not have love, we can do nothing with all this power.

I will give to the poor and even give up my body to be burned (as do some of those wishing to be martyrs of mankind who have literally set themselves aflame for causes or for sacrifices), and I do not have love, I have gained nothing. When I do things without love then I do them for the wrong reasons.

Love suffers so very long for others and is so very kind. Love does not envy others. Those who love are not proud or arrogant and go about trying to let the world see how great they are.

Love doesn't behave badly or unacceptably and does not seek possessions for itself. It keeps coming back courageously to serve others because it is not easily discouraged.

Love rejoices; has great joy for truth and virtue.

Believe. Bear up, hope and endure!

Love will never let you down. Everything can fall apart; the world can crumble about you, but if you have love, you will be able to go on. All earthly possessions, even to all knowledge, will cease to be one day and return to the dust of the earth, but not love!

We know only a part of the greatness of what love brings —

But when Jesus comes again, we will know the whole and then we will know the rapture of total love in its purest form.

Marriage partners cannot truly be called partners if they are so driven to hurting one another that they fail to love. All too often the hurt does not stop with the partners; it extends into the lives of those with whom they are closest — children, parents, friends, neighbors.

How can we assure that we *can* hurt one another? First, we can assure our mates that we are a narcissist. That is, that we love ourselves first and foremost. "This is my car, this is my apartment, this is my body!" Ever heard that before? You can probably say that you have. I don't suppose any of my younger readers have ever seen what happens when you pair a team of two mules together who haven't been teamed up before. Talk about a mess! We had two mules like that on our farm and ranch when I was growing up. Each one wanted to go his own direction and even the best "skinner" (driver) couldn't get them to perform. Not only would they wear themselves out, they tore up the equipment and messed up the ground. This may be a strong illustration, but this is what it is like in the pairing of two selfish, do-your-own-thing individuals. Maybe the mule illustration isn't too strong as it paints a more vivid picture. The values we express in this type of "religion of self" are the values that will not be conducive to a relationship which depends upon service, patience, kindness, and commitment.

Second, set up a barrage of mental abuse. Criticize daily, focus blame and call your partner names.

Third, keep the conflicts going by putting your partner in a "no-win" position. Tell your partner you don't like it when he goes fishing with his friends, then complain if he is "under foot" when you have some friends over. Demand that he take you out to eat once in a while, then complain about the places he suggests.

Fourth, cease communicating. Talk all you want to but don't dare communicate. There are some scriptures in the Old Testament on women who talk incessantly or who badger with words. "A continual dropping on a very rainy day and a contentious woman are alike" (Proverbs 27:15).

Fifth, fail to be together. Why anyone knows that when people are together they can become mischievous and unruly. But how about the power? Jesus needed to appoint disciples and He never sent them out alone (Mark 6:7, Luke 10:1) to face their commissions, and we know that He told us to fellowship one another (Matthew 18:19-20). Jesus wanted His disciples with Him when He was praying (Mark 10:32). When a husband and wife are truly together in thought and deed, they begin to have the association in which they will learn humility and patience which are two valuable assets to character to enable them to "make it" in marriage. We can become genuine partners when we pray together and pull *together*. Self-centeredness disappears when we have togetherness.

Finally, just tear the book of Romans, 12th chapter from your Bible. Without this chapter there you won't have to be reminded of your responsibility and commitment.

I have just used the negative introduction to bringing your attention to steps which could lead your marriage into ultimate destruction.

Please be sure to reverse each of these steps and work toward building a lasting relationship; to stop hurting and start loving.

Strange that the heart of all emotion and feeling, both mental and physical, in a word (love) is so undefinable. All of us could flip to a definition in a dictionary and come out with a line or two that would enable us to write or recite a meaning, but this would not encompass the strength and power of the word 'love.' Some people struggle an entire lifetime accomplishing great feats just to hear the echo from another's lips, "I love you, or we love you." These unfortunate people sometimes are never able to hear these words because those who are closest to them or who deserve them are stingy with approval and love.

When we love someone we are caring, feeling, ever-watchful, adjusting and readjusting, listening and really hearing, pleasing, and serving that person.

As much as we differ, we are alike. We will have the poor souls who do not have love with us always and yet we can try to reach them by remembering them in love in their condition and not despise them for their lack of love. Through lack of contact with God and godly persons, these people never learned to love; we should say to ourselves, "but for the grace of God, there go I." As infants they came here with the same feelings, the same emotions, and with prayer for them, we can hope that someday they should feel in their hearts and learn to truly love with agape love.

Ever wake up some morning or have a stray thought as this: "Why in the world did I marry him? We have no common ground, we are opposites, totally different. We will never be able to grow in harmony."

I am sure that many of us have had those thoughts. This is where the work comes in. I believe this is the beginning of selfish thinking and we should remember 1 Corinthians 10:24, 32, 33, where Paul talks about not seeking our own good, but the good of others. You married him because you loved him and wanted to share your life with him, but for a moment there you were forgetting the goal of love in marriage that love seeks not its own (1 Corinthians 13:5). At this time require yourself to give that love you promised 'til death parts you.' Then go on reading the 13th chapter of 1 Corinthians and you will find that the devil has set his course on your heart and unless you truly work at putting self last, and your feelings on being totally different, you will be unable to grow in harmony; instead you will grow apart.

When my boys were small they would fall and sustain a bad "Bobo" (our name for an abrasion) and they would run to me saying,

94

"It hurt." This was my sign to kiss the hurt away. The boys did this because: (1) I had played a little touching game with physical hurts when they were very small and they thought it actually worked; (2) they felt I would feel their hurt and sympathize with them; (3) they associated love and affection with the easing of hurting and pain. We know that *loving* does ease the *hurting*.

Touching or physical embracing, a sign of loving, can ease the hurting in life. When I have my feelings badly abashed from time to time, all it takes to soothe them is for my husband to reach out and take me in his arms and hug me and the hurt is eased, or erased, and the slate is clean. This sign of his still loving is my sign to stop hurting.

We should practice hurting less and loving more. If we practiced loving as children, as friends, as brothers and sisters, mothers and fathers, as well as husbands and wives, then we would perform loving signs more often and with more efficiency. We would have our antennas out to perceive the hurt, realize it for what it is and how we managed to hurt, then set about to correct by the love.

How many times does pride interfere with admission of a wrong to the other party. There have been many times when I let pride interfere with apologies and I know that my husband has done the same thing and just as I have wished I had not, when I reflect, I know he has also reflected and wished that he had not been so proud. You know why? We both see how many good times we missed by being so foolish in our youth when we were playing "stand-off."

Is it that we believe we are punishing our mates when we fail to relieve the hurt by the love? That's what it appears to be. We say to ourselves, "So, he's going to do thus and so . . . well, I'll show him!" See the round shoulder moving — it flips around nicely. So we shrug off all the pain and hurt, begin building a wall around our feelings and let them boil inside and then we begin to hurt and punish our mate. We begin to destroy the relationship because we are recalling and punishing, and not forgetting and forgiving.

All our hurting, loving, making it does not center upon husbands and wives and their personal and interpersonal relationships, but encompasses hurting and loving when we deal with others who pass through our lives and our relationships with them. This certainly concerns our children. Just as our mate becomes our victim, so do others. Our children learn to hurt and love just as we hurt and love. Sometimes they get the two very mixed up because their models (their parents) have gotten them so mixed up. As I wrote earlier, we can look at our children and see ourselves mirrored. I wonder why? We can see them spiraling down the road of life just as we spiraled

95

before them. They are indeed our left-handed image. When my dear sweet husband and I see our boys make the same mistakes that we made, when we see the foolishness of their actions, we only see the foolishness of what we had been and we know that they learned this from us. God purposed that none should hurt and that all should love properly that we would see the foolishness of our not being able to through the actions of our children — what better way to teach.

As mentioned before, I suppose I have had as many hurts concerning my children as most parents, only the hurts were "colored" differently. I should not like to state exactly what these hurts were as it would be a violation of confidences which only our family shared. But God provided us with whatever resources we needed to handle our problems when they arose when we appealed to Him. God promised us that He would give us no more than we could bear (1 Corinthians 10:13). Through this realization and promise, I have survived some very difficult traumatic times. I am sure that my husband would not mind my mentioning one example as it occurs so commonly that it's effect on the ego is not all consuming. He was a successful coach and yet he was fired from his coaching job. Nowadays, that is a common thing which happens to coaches. Then, it happened, but somehow or the other one never feels like it will happen to him, and it was a more traumatic event as jobs were harder to find in coaching. I was home in bed with the flu the day he called me to write up a face-saving letter of resignation. After discussing this together at length, we decided that this would be a hypocritical step and so we faced the option of being publically disgraced. As the news appeared in the newspapers, everyone hushed talking when we came around, our real neighbors and family consoled us, our coaching friends and co-workers deserted us and did not want to be seen talking or visiting with us. Thus, a 13-year career ended because my husband allowed it to end; he could have been reemployed a dozen times over because there were job offers, but it was as if he climbed into a shell and sank into a depression. No matter how hard I tried, he would not discuss his feelings. He was never told why and knowing why meant a lot to him. To this day, the reason why remains a secret. I felt it was because he was caught up in

a larger scheme of things and it was easier for those wanting a complete change over in coaching faculty to ignore the questions because there were no good reasons why. The children were teased at school about this and you are the "son of a has-been," or you are getting to play 1st string because you "old man" was a coach here (not because he was the best the team had in that position). The hurt and sting of the whole mess went on for years and I guess, inadvertently we are still affected by it, although my dear, sweet Christian husband was able to overcome his feelings and bitterness and learn to cope. I was very grateful when he was no longer the empty shell he had become after that. As God would have it, it was for the best as he went on to a better job and a realization that the period of coaching had aggravated a pre-existing heart condition and as an end result the problem was diagnosed early enough to prevent a heart attack. Tell me God doesn't answer prayers! God was allowing Satan to use my husband's superiors and "friends" to do His will. He allowed all of this to take place, and what looked like a game of chess with a person's life to an outsider, became a maneuver of salvation to my mate. He then became a deacon of the church and later an elder.

Two years after finding out about his heart condition I, too, succumbed to some problems which I had dismissed too lightly, only to find out that I would also have to ease off a bit because I had a mitral valve prolapse. I talked to God and He gave me the solution by helping me keep my zeal for life as energetically as I had always. My talents multiplied and as I continued to grow, I grew to love. God closed a door and He opened a window. Can't you just see Satan, sighing and crying over all this, and God smiling and loving. And like the old villain of the "Batman" series, Satan was "foiled again."

I suppose I could relate 100 incidents where I could specifically see how we hurt in our lives, but neither space nor time will allow, and perhaps these incidents would show you that you are not alone out there. However, if you will use the chapter questions, you will be motivated to search your hearts for signs of hurting and then get busy and search the scripture and do something about loving away the hurt.

Loving means focusing on attributes and not focusing on faults or failings. We all know we have faults, even the most vain of us, but then most mentally healthy people feel they have a lot of good things going for them. Forget about loving "if my mate did this or that for me, I could really love him." Recall a famous line from J. F. Kennedy, "Ask not what your country can do for you, but what you can do for your country." Apply that to "ask not what he can do for me, but what can I do for him." A woman may say to her husband or about her husband, "I love him because he understands me," or three short, simple words, "I love you."

When we begin examining ourselves closely and see why it is hard for us to love others as we should, I think we begin to understand that what we see in others that we dislike so much are perhaps those characteristics which we despise in ourselves. Just as we cannot become loving people overnight, we cannot learn all the attributes of how to love overnight. However, if we move closer to God daily, He will teach us to love.

There are many clue words related to one root word — love. When we truly have learned to love one another, loving begins and it does not end until we die. As Paul wrote in Ephesians 5:25: "husbands, love your wives as Christ loved the Church and *gave* himself to her." God *gave* His only son (John 3:16). Christ loved His church and *gave* His life (Ephesians 5:25). God commanded us to *give* and through the *giving* we would learn the *loving*.

I cannot almost hear and see Moses when he was trying to counsel all his followers as they wandered in the wilderness, "Can't you people get your act together! Quit hurting one another, love one another. Live by God's laws." Moses finally had to appoint counselors to help him out. The bitterness and the hurting screamed out against the marriage partners. The hurt was so far removed from the love that the partners often could not be nourished back to conjugation. So, the married partners progressed to further hurting.

The psyche can be fed by yourself or others. If someone is hurting, generally that person will seek out another who is also hurting in trying to find love and he/she may even find more hurt. Married people who have gradually descended steps that could have led to a successful marriage, did so because they were inept at loving. Lack of loving can be called by many names but whatever the name becomes, it started out being "lack of love." From all my dealings with others and from reading and studying, I feel like those who have found themselves separated or divorced, found themselves in this condition because of lack of love.

Tell me what I can do, you say. Well, many things can be done to putting a marriage on the right course, even when it has reached the lawyer's office. Remember, "I can do all things through God who strengtheneth me." Use everything God has put at your disposal, honestly, and express love positively. Use your talents to reach the taste buds by providing good meals. Stay clean in spirit and heart. Take a look in the mirror and without being vain make yourself beautiful with good grooming and caring about your appearance at all times. The sound of a soft voice can turn away anger, and the sound of beautiful music can lift the spirit. Touch the one you love as touching indicates closeness and involvement. Did I touch upon the adage that the way to a man's heart is through his stomach? Well, maybe. We all know that it requires more than the basics of reaching the senses to keep a marriage together. However, this is a beginning and when you are doing these things you will certainly do no damage to the relationship and you will be following God's commandments.

When you make up your mind to stop hurting remember that you (1) do not use the old hurts and old grudges as weapons; (2) do not talk about others and compare their successes to your failures; and (3) do not dwell on faults of yours or others.

Our partners should never be abused mentally by hateful mannerisms, unkind remarks, jokes at their expense, or ridicule at their attempts to please, for this abuse will surely be initial and finalizing steps to marital rifts. When we hurt others, we only demonstrate how little we think of ourselves and we can enjoy no inner peace or love completely. Through God we can change our lives for God is love and whoever lives in love, lives in God and God lives in Him (1 John 4:16).

When we find ourselves hurting and it ends up with us on opposite sides, back-to-back, on a king-size bed, then we should remember that we are not to let the sun go down on our wrath (Ephesians 4:26). We may leave this earth in that condition!

Refer to scriptures on submission (1 Corinthians 13:5-8), be unselfish (1 Corinthians 7:4), and always care for others (Philippians 2:4). If we lived by these scriptures, rebellion and desire to hurt would diminish because it is impossible to love God and be His servant and still experience the characteristics of malice, jealously, hatred, deception, indifference, inadequacy, rage, shame, envy, which causes us to hurt others. Hatred of enemies is not possible either (1 Corinthians 13:4, Matthew 5:44). In Romans 12:17-21, Paul states that evil should not repay evil, and people should live peaceably with all people. How can we make such a mess of our home lives and go out and seek to live peaceably with the world and all mankind.

Love can be learned. It's never too late because people yearn for acceptance and love their entire lifetimes. While I was getting my Masters in Counseling and Guidance, I had to do much study on studies done on love and psychological well-being. I remember one in which infants were divided into groups; with one group being touched and talked to and held, and the other given very little attention, except for necessary attention during feeding and changing or medical care. You can guess the group with the most deaths by the age of two. I also studied, which interestingly enough disputes honest statistics, theories of scientists of the mind who do not credit love with the power it truly has upon the lives of those who practice love in its proper form. These scientists called love that was unselfish as love that was delusionary, idealistic or obsessive. Recently medical doctors have found that it is helpful in the healing of physical hurts and sicknesses that patients respond better when their doctors show tenderness by their care and touching their patients gently on the arm or forehead. It was found that these patients got better quicker or accepted terminal illnesses more readily.

Love is the following:

1. Sharing instead of selfishness
2. Giving instead of taking
3. Patient instead of impatient
4. Serving instead of unserving
5. Accepting instead of rejecting
6. Hoping instead of hopeless
7. Responsible instead of irresponsible
8. Tolerant instead of intolerant
9. Forgiving instead of unforgiving
10. Humble instead of vain
11. Respectful instead of disrespectful
12. Strong instead of weak
13. Unique instead of common
14. Understanding instead of misunderstanding
15. Kind instead of unkind
16. Beautiful instead of ugly

Just as we learn to love, we learn to hurt. The more experiences we get in hurting, the more proficient we become in hurting. Learn to live and grow in love until skills are perfected. Always think in the present tense — I love, you love, not I *was* loving. Love is forever in the present tense and how we loved yesterday decides how we love today and how we love today decides how we will love tomorrow. I capture the beauty of a springtime bloom with my camera, and years later I look with anticipation at the subject captured in celluloid, but I find I cannot recapture the inward feeling that I once had when I initially beheld the bloom with all its radiance. I had managed to keep the image, but it did not lift my spirits as it once had. Nations are oppressed and people in these nations may lose their will to choose; man is oppressed and he often loses his will to love. Nations and men lose the ability to feel love as they lost their will to love.

Love is something if you give it away, give it away . . . it comes back to you. Love is one thing we do not have to seek — it finds. Give it and others will be drawn to you.

Hold your arms out for a child indicating that you wish to have that child come to you. Your arms are open — the child knows he comes to love. When you call to a child with folded arms, the child knows you are angry. The child's arms are still outstretched; he still wants the love and begins to cry because he knows it will be denied him. As adults, we use the same techniques. We play the game — more hurting — less loving.

This book truly has no end, because just as I instruct you to work diligently to assure that you make it, I too, will continue to do the same. Neither space nor time will allow all the incidents that would tell you that you are not alone out there. However, if you will use the chapter and questions, you will be motivated to search your hearts for signs of hurting and then get busy — do something about loving away the hurt. And with that I leave some prose I penned to you entitled *The Magic of Love.*

> The magic of love,
> Given only from my God above
> *whispers* to the tiny baby,
> Hush, don't cry and
> gently soothes the tears away.
>
> *Speaks* to the blue-jeaned youngster,
> Come, I'll kiss and
> tosses affectionately the tufts of hair.
>
> *Shouts* to the young teen,
> Hey, Let's hug and
> slaps lovingly the shoulder
>
> *Smiles* to the aging one,
> Nods, eyes glittering and arms outstretched,
> holds the other near.
>
> *Screams* to the hurting
> Help, my God above
> Powerfully spin the magic of love.

Sequel

Be assured that I do not rest on my laurels — until the day God takes me away from my beloved, I will be working hard at "Making

It," fighting the sin of which I am guilty and overcoming Satan, and then when I meet God at His throne and He directs me to His right side, He will say to me, "My child, you have defended the cause of Christ; you were committed; you have made it!"

Chapter XII

Study Questions

1. How can we assure that we will not hurt others?

2. List some sure ways of hurting those you love. Discuss.

3. Write down 3 things you have prayed for in the last year and put them aside. Write down the dates you prayed or extended time you prayed for these things. In the future, write down dates and how you saw your prayers were answered.

4. Face up to your weaknesses. Write down 3 instances which occurred whereby you hurt your mate, your child, or another person. These people did not tell you of this, but you came to the realization yourself of your actions.

5. What should be done about this list? Write the solutions out to the side of each instance.

Chapter XIII

CONCLUSION

There are many factors which mold our character so that we are more able to make marriage work which deserve some mention that have not been covered thus far. One of these is the witnessing and forming of loving relationships with others as children grow into adults. The person who said that we learn what we live was right.

One of the experiences of my life which I attribute some of the abilities attained in gaining sensitivity to the needs of others and to the development of my character to feel love deeply was in a close association and affection of grandparents. I had great grandparents who were devoted to one another and to their families, although these grandparents had very short lives. My grandmother on the maternal side was a paraplegic from the age of 3, yet she married and gave birth to seven children, whom she raised with zest and vitality and with as much normalcy as possible. She was never helpless and was a contributor to all the normal routine of the family life, even though she got about in a straight chair which she walked using her shoulder strength to perform her household tasks. Grandpa was a devoted and serving mate, tender and gentle in his behavior toward Grandma. He was also one who took time to stop and admire the beautiful things around him in life and taught me to do the same. I remember well an incident which occurred while he lived with us after Grandma's death.

Sumac twines its way around the Mayhaw trees and fence rails in southwestern Louisiana and has a perfectly lovely orange and red blossom. On a walk through the pasture with Grandpa, to get the milk cows, the sumac caught my eye. Oh, I wanted one of those beautiful blossoms so badly that I told Grandpa to get it for me. He knew the danger that would come by his obtaining the bloom for me, but he carefully gathered and trimmed away several of the stems and held them out for me to admire. And in doing so, he said, "all that is beautiful and desired of the eye is not always best for you." He told me about the sumac and its poison to the skin and he suffered the painful rash and the consequences of his act for days, just to bring a few moments of joy to a granddaughter and at the same time teach a value lesson.

I also remember the pain that that same Grandpa suffered as he built a homemade casket that was to hold his beloved mate when death took her from him at the age of 56.

Agape love is controlled by determination, not by emotion. Jamie Welch was never told by Carlile that she was loved, and yet he wrote, "Oh, if I had you yet, but one hour, that I might tell you all."

I wrote a book once, called *A Touch of Velvet*, in which I told the story of a slave who had been freed, but who gave up his freedom to work for the freedom of a negress whom he loved. It was based on a true story which happened in Louisiana before the Civil War times. What was very evident to me was that this slave had been taught the Bible because his story paralleled the story of Jacob and Rachel of the Old Testament (Genesis 29:20). Jacob loved Rachel and he worked for seven years for Laban to receive his wish. Now Jacob's life would not be all that long that he would be willing to sacrifice this much of it, but he did, and he did it willingly so that it seemed like the shortest period of his life. Why does time fly so quickly when one has a goal and works cheerfully towards that goal? The answer can be found in the fact that love is able to make time fly. But you say, Jacob lived 147 years and he could well afford to give up only 7 years! and I say, *but for love, one would not be willing to give anything up, let alone 7 years.*

Some say that it is impossible to reach the highest form of love — agape love. Pity those. We know it's possible. Most mothers reach this state more readily with their children than with the others in their lives. We have seen mothers who stand at the very edge of despair, knowing that their wonderful, marvelous children have grown into hardened criminals who have committed heinous acts against mankind, waiting and weeping in both sorrow and in love for those children, now adult, still loving the child they were, still forgiving the person they have become, but never understanding their actions. Is this not akin to the type of love which God expects of us? Evidence has proved that not all the mothers are able to come to the point of putting out the effort that it takes to build that kind of love. In this type of love the mother feels every pain, every hurt that comes to the lives of her children and she would gladly trade places and suffer for her children if she could. She has an empathy which far exceeds sympathy. This mother is placing her family's welfare before her own — she is a worthy person in the eyes of her family; she is a worthy person in her own eyes; she is so spiritual that she never feels personal threats for her submissiveness to her family. She feels right about herself and would have her life no other way. She is free, inwardly, and yet is an obedient servant and carries no grudge of her service to others in her family for she is not "in servitude."

As a public high school teacher, I had the privilege of listening to a lectureship by Harris, who wrote the book *I'm Okay, You're Okay*, and many of the things he expressed about an individual's worth, which we should feel as Christians, are almost paraphrased from the Bible. They could have just as easily been Jesus' words about personal worth. The whole clue to our being able to make it as friends and neighbors of others is found in the basic truth of being able to make it with ourselves.

Marital relationships are affected by many contributing factors other than those mentioned in this work. Some of these are jobs, bad habits, careers, moves from city to city, state to state, states to foreign countries, societal changes, lack of family togetherness and tradition, differing value systems. However, even in facing the problems I have mentioned, as well as those just listed, it is possible to make your marriage work, but you must work at your marriage. If married couples would work as hard at their marriages as they do at their professions or even their hobbies, then marriages would work which otherwise might fail.

Remember that the summer of your life quickly fades into fall and opportunities to change, to do what is right, to be that special mate, will slip away. God intends that marriage is to be a lifetime contract (Romans 7:1-4), and no man or woman should put away his/her mate except for reason of marital unfaithfulness (fornication, Matthew 19:9). So, we *must* keep on "keeping on." Winter has its joys. The snow of winter caps the highest mountains, and the heavy ice causes the bending of the most stately oaks — these acts are performed and lend dignity with their covering. And so it is with the age of man. Age turns the raven hair to glistening white, and the weight of stressful burdens contours the strongest body to fit its load. With age comes wisdom — to cover the loss of one attribute, we gain another and this wisdom gained from age should not be wasted. Proverbs 23:22 states: "Harken unto thy father that begat thee, and despise not thy mother when she is old," for through the wisdom of another's trials, we learn. When you hear the voices of the future call to you "times have changed and to stay married is old-fashioned," remember that what God said was "good" will never be old fashioned, for He saw man's motives before He created him.

God considered the creation of man and women partnership as being "very good." He was very proud of what He had created. He saw no reason why there should not be mental and physical harmony.

A growing empathy prevails in the feelings of my mate and I. We let each other know that our lives and work are important to each other, and most of all, is that we share a lifelong partnership with God. We truly are best friends; we truly do have agape love, because the love shines through all the ugly, the unhelpful, the triteness, the unpleasantness, and finds the glow of the lovely and beautiful, the helpful, the simplicity, the pleasant and as . . .

A friend is one
who knows you
as you are

Understands where
you've been
Accepts who you've
become
and still
gently
invites
you to
grow . . .

—*Quoted (author not given)*

such is the way of our friendship.

Even to your old age
I am he
and even to hoar hairs
I will carry you:

106

I have made you,
and I will bear;
even I will carry,
and will deliver you.

—Isaiah 46:4

Chapter XIII

Study Questions

1. Relate cheerfulness in attitudes to goals in life.
2. What does love have to do with giving? (This is a short question, but it calls for an expansive answer.)
3. Define Agape love.
4. Relate service to God to service to man.
5. Relate service to husbands to submissiveness. Tie this in with agape love.
6. How important is the "you" to the "other" in being able to make it in life?
7. Discuss the thought "people are not islands."
8. Name some contributors (factors which affect) marital relationships.
9. Read Romans 7:1-4; Matthews 19:9. Discuss.
10. Read Proverbs 23:22. Relate this to your studies in this book.

BIBLIOGRAPHY

Browning, Robert. "Calm Repose," *Rabbi Ben Ezra.*

Choate, Betty Burton. "Growing Old in Love," *Love Poems,* 1985.

Guenther, Louis H. "Life's Seasons," Salesian Mission Booklets, 1984.

Kipling, Rudyard, "If," *The Home Book of Verse,* ed. by Burton Egbert Stevenson, New York: Henry Holt and Company, 1945, p. 2951. (7th edition)

Luther Martin. Quote from Elaine Steman's book, *A Woman's Worth,* Waco, TX: Word Book, Inc., 1975.

Modern Secretary. Editorial Release by Dr. Robert Lauer, United States Int. Univerisity, San Diego, CA, November, 1984, p. 9.

"People Quiz," *Family Weekly,* for Lake Charles American Press, February 22, 1981.

Rice, Helen Steiner. "The Meaning of True Love," *The Greatest of These Is Love,* compiled by Donald T. Kauffman for Random House, N.Y.

Small, Dwight Hervey. *Marriage as Equal Partnership.* Ann Arbor, Mich.: Baker Book House Co., 1980, pp. 58-59.

Stevenson, Robert L. *An Evening Prayer,* New York: Barse and Hopkins, Pub., 1895.

Stinnett, Nick. *20th Century Christian.* July, 1981, Vol. 43.

The Holy Bible. King James Version. Nashville, TN: The Nashville Bible House

The Living Bible. Wheaton, Illinois: Tyndale House Publishers, 1976.

The 20th Century Christian. editorial section. July 1981, p. 9, Vol. 43.

Vine, W. E. *An Expository Dictionary of W. T. Words*, N. J.:
Fleming H. Revell Co., 1966.